EXPLORING an ALIEN CULTURE

What can we learn from the Vikings, Scandinavian Immigrants and Nordic People Today?

by J.B. Hove

Juel Publishing
Isanti, MN

Cover: Raoul Wallenberg's image is a June 1944 passport photo by Hagströmer & Qviberg. Johanna Sigurdardottir's 2009 portrait is from Iceland's Ministry of Social Issues. Ingrid Bergman was photographed by A.L. Whitey Schafer in 1940. N.F.S. Grundtvig's image was painted by Christian Albrecht Jensen in 1831. The date and photographer of Alfred Nobel's picture are both unknown. Fridtjof Nansen's 1915 portrait by Henry van der Weyde was purchased by the U.S. government from the George Grantham Bain Collection in 1948. Sigrid Undset's portrait was from an unknown artist at an unknown date. Niels Bohr's image is from his 1922 Nobel Prize photo. Tarja Halonen's portrait was provided by the Office of the President of the Republic of Finland. Jean Sibelius' picture is from "What We Hear in Music" by the Victor Talking Machine Co. in 1913. Some of these photos were obtained through Wikimedia Commons.

Juel Publishing
28265 Strike Blvd NW
Isanti, MN 55040

ISBN: 978-0-9793762-1-4

First Edition
Printed in the United States of America
Copyright © 2013 by J.B. Hove

Unattributed translations are by the author.

Contents

Preface

A long-time passion for books, redirected by a sudden interest in family history (after my father's death in 1988) prompted me to read Scandinavian histories, travelogues, fiction, archeology texts, genetics studies, biographies, Icelandic sagas, Jordanes, mythology—anything that might provide clues about my ancestors. An unanticipated by-product of this reading was a 2007 book, *From Scandinavian Shores*, which attempted to describe the unique shared heritage of Scandinavian immigrants.

It might be helpful to note that two books were the catalyst for *FSS: Early Life* by Swedish American cleric Eric Norelius (an autobiography), and *Norse-Folk* by American clergyman Charles Loring Brace (an 1856 Nordic travelogue). Both authors described Nordic life from an American perspective (as outsiders). Researching and writing *FSS* took a decade, and before it was done, I was hooked on culture.

My wife, Linda, and I first visited Norway and Sweden (plus two days in Copenhagen) in 1990. We were lucky to be able to stay with second cousins who graciously entertained us and guided us to where our ancestors had lived. Our roots experiences were unforgettable but there were other experiences.

Whatever my preconceived notions were, I was struck by how modern and neat everything was. For example, I still remember looking at my cousin's home and noticing the steel roof—very expensive construction at home. He and his wife lived out in the country, and all of the farm machinery that we saw appeared to be very up-to-date; nothing looked old or dilapidated. And he had goldenrod planted in his garden. I had been taught that goldenrod was a weed, but he was intentionally growing it.

By staying with Linda's cousin's family we continued our education. Observing her mother's cousins, Linda said that she "finally understood her own mother." Sometimes the younger members of our host family had an in-your-face directness that I had never experienced at home.

Before returning in 2002 we twice visited elsewhere in Europe. We spent two weeks in the UK including six days visiting with locals and staying at inns. And we took a two-week guided tour of central and southern Europe.

In 2002 we were again able to stay with relatives and friends in Sweden and Norway, two of whom had lived in the United States and were aware of differences between America and their homeland. This time, I took every opportunity to visit bookstores searching for anything that might shed some light on Nordic people, returning home with a suitcase full of books.

In 2008 we visited Sweden briefly but focused on Finland where we were most fortunate, staying five days with a friend who was a retired teacher and who had lived in the United States for a year. This time we used only public transportation; it amazed me that one could carry on a normal conversation, or easily get up and walk around, on a train traveling 100 miles per hour.

In 2009 we visited Denmark, attempting to see as much as possible relating to culture, history, and archeology. It was September, the weather was less than ideal, and everywhere we saw children outside, either with parents or teachers.

These four visits totaled little more than two months, but they left impressions. Corresponding with Nordic friends for decades has left impressions. Visiting with literally thousands of people, while doing book promotions at various Scandinavian festivals, has left impressions. For example, occasionally women would tell me that they could "feel" higher status when they visited a Nordic country. But the biggest impression I received from talking to Scandinavian descendants is that they imagine whatever they have observed is probably unique to their family or unique to one Nordic country. These various impressions are not included with the references, but they influenced this text.

However, these trips to Scandinavia and visits with descendants of the immigrants are not significant sources for this book; instead it is based on the recorded observations of others. Readers are encouraged to refer to the documented sources. It is significant where information (or an idea) comes from; the background of the source is significant, and all of the sources deserve credit—they are the foundation of this book. Of course, these sources are in no way responsible for my errors and omissions.

This writer's efforts might be compared to an early twentieth-century anthropologist who lived with and observed some remote people on the other side of the earth and who attempted to make sense of those observations. Except, this is the twenty-first century and the people being observed are Nordic people, and they are being "observed" through written and other sources over a long time.

The early twentieth-century anthropologist likely believed that his own values, which he did not fully comprehend, were superior to those of the people he was studying. He had positive or negative (or both) feelings about the people he was observing. He was not a clean slate; when he began his observations, he had expectations about what he would find. But when he wrote up his study, he assumed a posture of detached impartiality, as if his own values and expectations had no effect on his conclusions.

This writer is not impartial or detached. To pretend otherwise would be dishonest. But most of the evidence presented here can be verified by accessing the references, and there has been a conscious effort to realistically interpret sources and to avoid distortions.

Today in America it is common for graduate students to explore in fine detail subjects that often have little relevance outside of academia. The goal of this book is just the opposite: I have attempted to define and illuminate (what I believe to be) important elements of culture with just enough detail to sharpen the focus. Readers who need more detail will often find it by referencing the sources.

A brief outline might be useful: Chapter One attempts to define culture; Chapter Two explains the general theme (argument); Chapters Three through Ten explore evidence for eight different elements (or facets) of culture; Chapter Eleven compares twenty Nordic, European, and English-speaking countries on various "progress indexes"; Chapters Twelve and Thirteen compare Nordic and American cultures; and Chapter Fourteen reviews elements of Nordic culture in contrast with relevant American culture.

There is no intent to slight any people or countries that were not included here. It seems natural to compare Nordic countries with their neighbors (other European countries), and readers would, no doubt, be curious where the United States and Canada fit in. Countries such as Japan, Singapore, South Korea, and others may rank high, even first, on some progress indexes, but those countries are beyond the scope of this effort, and this writer is uninformed about culture in those countries. No disrespect is intended.

1

An Alien Culture

*Too much importance is attached to
laws and too little to mores [culture].*

—Alexis de Tocqueville

The forty-two radio telescopes on California's Mount
Shasta (featured in the movie *Contact* starring Jodie Foster)
were designed to listen to radio waves for evidence of
intelligent life elsewhere in the Milky Way galaxy. A telescope
and other equipment are currently being used to detect laser
pulses (light) that might have been sent out by intelligent
life outside of earth. NASA's Kepler space telescope is
searching for evidence of earth-like or "habitable" planets
beyond our solar system. Satellites, probes, and telescopes
are searching for water or other possible evidence that life
might exist, or could have existed, elsewhere in the solar
system. Worldwide, hundreds of scientists are exploring
space for evidence of extraterrestrial (alien) life.

What would happen if any of this exploration produced
convincing evidence of extraterrestrial life? If that occurred,

our media would be saturated with details of the new evidence, including simple descriptions of the technology involved and interviews with scientists. These scientists would point out that their explorations had often subsisted on donations or insufficient funding, but now—with evidence in hand—it would be time to seriously fund their projects. In the face of good evidence, most of the public would be almost as curious as the scientists. Politicians would likely approve new funding. Whether this funding and these efforts would ever, in any way, improve people's lives might be discussed, but curiosity (science) would be the deciding factor.

But what if there were a significant feature of life—an alien culture—here on earth that, except for occasionally being superficially acknowledged, has not been explored, but which appears to be closely connected with a society's level of success? What if, decade after decade, a people who shared a common culture scored at or near the top on almost every conceivable measure of progress (education, transparent democracy, health care, prosperity, human rights, aid to others, etc.)? Wouldn't scientists be interested in exploring that culture? Not really.

The people claiming the high ground on the progress indexes are known to Americans as Scandinavians but are otherwise the people of the Nordic countries (Denmark, Finland, Iceland, Norway, and Sweden as well as the Faeroe and Åland Islands). If Nordic people are more progressive than others, why isn't there more curiosity, more exploration of their culture?

Nordic culture has, no doubt, been ignored because there are fewer Nordic people than there are Russians, or

Germans, or Japanese, or Brits. However, if Nordic culture breeds progress, the fact that these countries are not large is no reason to ignore them. Another rationale given for why their culture is ignored is the common perception that the Nordic countries have homogenous populations (not much diversity). This is only partly true, as they have some diversity (including a significant number of immigrants), and besides, it is hard to imagine how diversity could significantly impact some measures of progress, for example, transparent democracy or gender equality.

The study of culture is itself hampered by political correctness. If we compare—the only way to measure—cultures, some countries are at or near the bottom; this process is viewed by some as being politically incorrect. Arrogance may be another factor. We Americans tend to believe that we are the greatest nation on earth; what could we possibly learn from a few little countries in far northern Europe?

But the most important reason for ignoring Nordic culture may be that culture itself is so difficult to grasp.[1] Psychology, economics, laws, and political history are straightforward and rock-solid compared to fuzzy, slippery, usually invisible culture. Because it is difficult to grasp, in other publications *culture* may be hidden in terms such as *traditions, mentality, state of mind, spirit, soul, national character, folkways, customs, core values, behavior blueprints/patterns/codes, societal norms, conventions, mores,* or *morals*.

We seldom (sometimes never) acknowledge culture, but it constantly influences us. It determines the way—usually without thinking—we act or how we react. It is a blueprint or road map guiding us through life. Culture is always intangible and difficult to grasp. Perhaps the only time it is visible is when we meet someone who does not share our culture: then we see it by contrast. We see (imagine) that a person with a different culture is uninformed, wrong, sinful, backward, or just different. An example of this is nudity. Nordic people (and other Europeans) find nothing unusual about nudity at a beach or in a sauna, but many Americans have a different attitude.

It can be easy to imagine that culture is not learned but intuitive or instinctive (nature rather than nurture). For example, Norwegian American author Thorstein Veblen wrote:

> The individual has certain bents, instincts, which decide what he will aim towards. . . . Men would like the next generation to do better; they prefer future goods to present goods . . . all men are able to understand the thesis that we should not squander the resources needed by the incoming generation. This is an abhorrence of waste . . . .[2]

Veblen was writing in the early twentieth century. Near the end of the twentieth century, many Americans were spending without regard to tomorrow or future generations. From our perspective a century later, it appears that Veblen was describing his own culture—it was learned and not instinctive.

What may convincingly appear to be instinct or intuition ("nature") may actually be culture ("nurture"). *Nature* relates to the hardwiring we are born with, but research indicates

4

that our hardwiring is often, to some extent, rewired by experiences and environment ("nurture").[3]

Notwithstanding the intense rivalry visible among Nordic countries today, culture has been and is remarkably uniform across the whole Nordic region.[4] But there are exceptions, individual variations, local variations, and changes over time. However, when contrasted with other Europeans, the culture differences among Nordic people appear insignificant.[5] Enumerating all of the variations and exceptions would render this book unreadable. Instead, minor differences will be ignored, and readers are asked to remember that everyone is not the same, culture can vary from region to region, and there are always exceptions—nothing is absolute.

[Culture is] a blueprint for behavior, what must be done, what should be done, what may be done and what we are not allowed to do.[6]

—*Magnus Persson*

Some authorities believe that we have free will: every child is free to adopt his or her own culture.[7] But children absorb culture the same way they absorb language—they acquire the culture and the language of the community they are raised in.

Besides free will, one might argue that there is insufficient evidence to prove that some elements of culture have endured for many centuries.[8] True enough, there is no proof, but there is evidence, and that is the subject of this book: to explore evidence of culture gathered from different time periods, and from diverse sources. Evidence can take many forms; it is not restricted to one form (for example, scientific experiments).[9]

One way to study culture is to question people, which has been done for decades by an international group, World Values Surveys; their ongoing and well-known study, *Human Beliefs and Values*, is mentioned repeatedly in these pages.[10] But there are issues relating to cross-cultural comparisons based on questions: people sometimes ignore their own values and instead give what they believe is the correct answer; questions must be translated and phrased so they mean the same thing in each culture; external circumstances are often different from one culture to the next; and, not infrequently, it is necessary to interpret the answers.

Managing (they cannot be eliminated) these issues requires someone who has *observed* each culture to be compared.[11] For example, on a 1960s' study of American and Norwegian college students, the answers to one question (#88) made it appear that Norwegian students were significantly more selfish than their American counterparts. In reality, the Norwegian students were expressing their value that each person is responsible for taking care of his- or herself.[12] This same value plays a less direct role in question A030 on the *Human Beliefs and Values* survey (mentioned later).

Throughout these pages there is an underlying assumption that culture is absorbed, unconsciously or consciously, by children from their parents, siblings, friends, teachers, and others, and that it is handed down generation after generation.[13] Culture does not operate in a vacuum; human nature (biology and psychology), environment (climate, resources, neighbors, etc.), religion, and politics all influence culture.[14] And, culture has inertia: it continues over time unless its course is altered by some force.

[I]f we believe we already have the truth, we will lose interest in obtaining those very insights which might lead us to an approximate understanding of the situation.[15]

—*Karl Mannheim*

This writer has absolutely no desire to offend any individual, people, country, or religion, but an honest examination of culture may occasionally seem offensive. For example, some readers may be offended by evidence or suggestions related to family values or Christianity. Some readers will question the political correctness of national comparisons. Some readers may—without thinking—reject evidence that challenges their own political assumptions. A few readers may find it impossible to believe that their own country is not first in every measure of progress. Regardless, these pages are worth reading only if they accurately describe relevant evidence.[16]

Up until 1950, it was common for educated writers to give "race" and "culture" (upper-class culture) credit for the "superiority" of a nation or a people. Racial and cultural superiority was the philosophical justification for European colonization of large areas of the earth.

Writers sometimes claim that a few powerful men have shaped the human experience. Some experts see "progress" as a linear movement clearly delineated by touchstones such as written language, state formation, divine-right kings, the Industrial Revolution, and so on. In the latter half of the twentieth century, economics was proposed as the be-all to explain differences between peoples and nations. Traditional history stressed the importance of wars, leaders, and political developments. Religious authors routinely attribute progress to events related to their own religion. All of these approaches generally assume top-down change. They imagine that elements of progress (for example, reading and writing) were introduced by the upper class or powerful individuals or governments or a religion. In this scenario, ordinary people (90 percent of the population) are passive, or they resist progress. A humorous example of top-down change:

> It would have been well for Sweden, if Gustav III had never visited Italy, he having brought back with him the seeds of demoralization.[17]
>
> —*Mathew Jones*

Sweden's morals (sexual mores) changed because of one visit to Italy by a Swedish king, or so an 1829 English visitor believed.

One assumption of this writer is that—routinely— change is bottom-up.[18] But bottom-up change is universally overlooked; for example, in 1800s' Russia, peasants who wanted their children to learn to read and write secretly hired teachers because both the czar and the upper class were against educating ordinary people.[19] For a present-day researcher, it is much easier to uncover Russian laws establishing schools than it is to find even meager evidence of ordinary people's efforts to educate their children. And, evidence that politicians and laws were influenced by ordinary people's attitudes and values receives scant attention in scholarly studies, including history.[20]

It is culture, not politics, that determines the success of a society.

—*Daniel Patrick Moynihan*

Two examples of the importance of culture are the American civil rights movement and the fall of the Berlin Wall. In American media, the fall of the Berlin Wall has been linked to the power struggle between the United States and the Soviet Union (i.e. the United States won the Cold War). German Federal President Horst Koehler had a different perspective. In his view, there had been earlier reforms in other eastern European countries, while at the same time East Germans had lost faith in their government because they believed the elections of May 1989 had been rigged, and their attitude toward their own government turned negative. There were increasing demands for reform, and in October 1989 in the city of Leipzig many tens of thousands of East Germans demonstrated against their government—a month later the Berlin Wall came down. If President Koehler is correct, this is an example of the importance of culture.[21] Ordinary East Germans brought down their government because it did not meet their expectations (values and attitudes).

The American civil rights movement illustrates culture. Before the 1950s, the attitude of Blacks toward their "place" in America had been mostly submerged and, with a few exceptions, was visible only in poetry, art, and music. There were laws—federal laws—that guaranteed Blacks the right to vote, to use public transportation, and so on, but these laws were not enforced. In the South at least, White values trumped federal law.

Starting in the 1950s southern Blacks increasingly voiced their long-submerged attitude by protesting in one way or another. The violence and threats of violence unleashed on the protesters did not silence them; instead more Blacks and a few Whites joined the protests. These people expressing their values (fighting injustice) combined with the sympathy they evoked in northern Whites forced the federal government to start enforcing laws that had long been in existence and also to pass new civil rights laws. Black attitude (culture) was the engine driving the American civil rights movement of the 1950s and 1960s.[22]

Culture has also affected religious change. The change from Catholic to Lutheran (the Reformation) was not uniform in Scandinavia. In Iceland there was resistance and bloodshed;[23] in Denmark–Norway some people welcomed the Reformation; but in Sweden–Finland there was little complaint against Catholicism. Here people's attitude was: "there is no reason to change, and we ought to decide this for ourselves." Swedish kings starting with Gustav Vasa gradually introduced the new religion. Change came from above, but because of the attitude of the Swedes and Finns, it was a seventy-year process.

Not so five centuries earlier in Russia where the ruler Vladimir studied different religions and chose (apparently, because it did not inhibit drinking) Orthodox Christianity. After he made his choice, Vladimir ordered that Russians be baptized or suffer the consequences.[24] Vladimir was able to force Russians—quickly—to change religion because of culture: Russians believed that it was natural and necessary that they should be subject to an absolute ruler, and they did not expect to be part of the decision-making process.[25]

Today, in some countries young women are murdered by their fathers or brothers because they have dishonored their family (so-called "honor killings"). In other countries— because of a different culture—these women's "crime," sex before marriage, would hardly be noticed.

One final insignificant example: if you were attending a neighbor's barbeque and the host handed you a burger, casually mentioning that it was horsemeat, would that affect your enjoyment of the burger? That's culture.

Culture is important—it does influence the course of individual lives, and it influences the progress of nations.[26] It does not get the attention it deserves because it is difficult to define, difficult to grasp, and difficult to test by traditional scientific methods.[27] Regardless of these difficulties, culture is trump.[28]

Curiosity was the driving force behind the research that went into this book, and curiosity is a good enough reason to read it. But there is another: Nordic culture works. Except for Norway's huge oil reserves, the Nordic countries are resource-deficient, but today they are at or near the top in almost any measure of progress, including prosperity. An understanding of Nordic culture has the potential to improve human lives.[29] But for some readers, both the concept that

11

our lives are ruled by culture and the idea that Nordic culture is significantly different—and more progressive—will be alien.

Nordic Culture: Respect others but
stand up for yourself and your values.[30]

2

Persistent Culture

[A]s Faulkner reminds us, the past is never
dead and buried—it isn't even past.[31]

—Barack Obama

Today, Denmark, Finland, Iceland, Norway, and Sweden
are world leaders in areas such as: transparent and responsive
democracy, human rights, women's rights, information and
other technology, urban planning, health care, education,
foreign aid, and prosperity. Countries are ranked on these
and other topics by various institutions: the Legatum
Institute (Prosperity Index), World Economic Forum
(various indexes), Organization for Economic Cooperation
and Development (various indexes for developed countries),
Reporters Without Borders (World Press Freedom Index),
World Bank (World Governance Indicators), United Nations
(Human Development Index), Transparency International
(government corruption), Center for Global Development
(Commitment to Development Index), Save the Children,
and others.[32]

Routinely, for "progress" topics such as those listed above, the Nordic countries rank in the top 10 percent, and often they rank in the top 5 percent. It is common for a Nordic country to be ranked number one in the world on one of these indexes. Whether the ranking is for 30 developed nations or for 160 nations around the world, the Nordic countries consistently rank near the top.

There is a riddle here: if persistent culture is responsible for present-day Nordic countries strong showing on progress indexes, why did millions of Scandinavians emigrate from 1825 to 1930? It is commonly imagined that they emigrated from countries that were backward and impoverished.

The answer lies in several factors: A rapidly expanding population throughout the 1800s, combined with a fixed land base and farm consolidation, meant that most children of Nordic landowners would never own their own land. At the same time, the transition from an agriculture-based economy to an industrial one did not create jobs fast enough to accommodate all of those displaced by farm consolidation. Free (or nearly so) land and good-paying jobs in the New World were powerful magnets.

Otherwise, compared to their neighbors, the Nordic countries during the emigration era were not impoverished. Scandinavian immigrants were poor by present-day American standards, but they left behind better homes, and they were not as poor as their contemporaries in England, Ireland, and other areas of Europe.[33]

A Swedish immigrant who later became a pastor in Wisconsin wrote of conditions he had observed during a one week layover in England in 1869:

I will never forget the misery and poverty, especially among the women and children. Such I had never seen in Sweden.[34]

—*Louis J. Ahlstrom*

In the Nordic countries—when necessary—people shared food, and in many places there was a formal welfare system.[35] When in the 1870s, this writer's great-great-grandparents (renters) became too old to work, the Swedish State Church auctioned caring for them to the lowest bidder.[36] They stayed together and were well cared for by a family who was reimbursed by the State Church. The same system was used when a husband died and left small children; then the children's care was auctioned to the lowest bidder (the mother if she thought she could do it alone). Vulnerable people were not necessarily abandoned.

[L]ook at the English peasantry and the German! How many cannot read or write! Here [1856, Sweden] it is very seldom that you will find a peasant who cannot read.[37]

—*Clergyman speaking to Charles Brace*

As the clergyman indicates, Swedish culture was progressive when it came to teaching people to read. Overall, Scandinavian immigrants (and Nordic people who didn't emigrate) were less backward—more modern—than their European contemporaries. Evidence supporting that argument will be explored in these pages. If the evidence is convincing, readers will not be surprised that the Nordic countries are, today, world leaders in progress, because they were also leaders in the past.

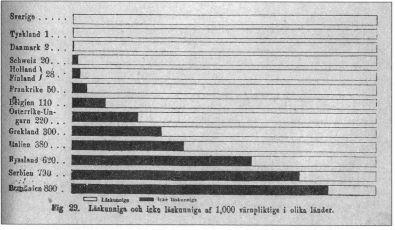

Fig 29. Läskunniga och icke läskunniga af 1,000 värnpliktige i olika länder.

Literacy among military conscripts

The above chart represents the number of men who could not read for each 1000 military draftees in fourteen European countries about 1880.[38] The countries are (from top to bottom) Sweden, Germany, Denmark, Switzerland, Netherlands, Finland, France, Belgium, Austria-Hungary, Greece, Italy, Russia, Serbia, and Romania. Education including literacy will be discussed later; this chart is significant here because more than 130 years ago the *relationship* between the Nordic countries and the other countries is similar to the *relationship* on the present-day progress indexes. The relationship is similar because of culture, or at least that is an argument to be defended in these pages.

The table below represents a simple contrast between the historical backgrounds in the Nordic region and non-

Central and southern Europe, Russia	Nordic region
Influences	**Influences**
Celtic, Slavic, Asian, and Mediterranean	Germanic, Finnic, nomadic herders
Longer growing season	Short growing season
Ample cropland	Limited cropland
Catholic & Orthodox	Lutheran after the Reformation
Unarmed ordinary people	Armed ordinary people
Large landowners	Large landowners
Little or no travel	Travel routine and necessary
Family or Village Identity	**Group Identity**
Patriarchal extended families	Nuclear families, indep. women
Married children dependent	Children independent early
Often, communal property	Generally, private property
Communal work	Cooperative work
Not responsible to "others"	Mutual responsibilities: fairness, justice, honesty
Strong patron–client ties	respect, truth-telling
Strong family ties	Weaker family ties
Family security	Social pressure, *Janteloven*
Authority	**Authority**
Patriarch has authority	People have authority
Landowner & prince have authority	King's authority from the people, a contract
No effective laws/institutions	Effective laws and institutions
Serfdom	Often, landowning peasants
Violent protest	Usually, legal/nonviolent protest
Idealistic	**Practical**
Religion (church) has authority	Religion separate; practical first
Meek acceptance, less planning	Organized, resourceful, *sisu*
Education unimportant	Children must be educated
Entertaining, idealistic literature	Realistic literature with message
Change is dangerous	Change is natural

17

Nordic areas of Europe. The differences to be explored in Chapters Three thru Ten might be easier to understand if readers refer to this table.

3

Independent Women

[1748] To us in Sweden, where the wife, no less than the husband, is obligated in everyway to bestir herself and keep her wits about her, to help win the necessities of life, an English wife would not seem particularly well suited.[39]

—Peter Kalm

Society's attitude toward women is a natural starting point for any discussion of Nordic culture: there is general agreement about this element of culture, it is easy to document, and there is a conceivable origin. It also influences other elements of culture. Because they often maintain family and social networks, because they apparently respond to challenges in different ways than men, and especially because they have more contact with young children, independent women influence culture.

Throughout these pages ordinary people (90 percent of the population) are the focus; it is especially important to acknowledge that while discussing women, because upper-

19

class women lived in a different world than ordinary women. For example, Henrik Ibsen's *A Doll's House* is written from an upper-class Norwegian perspective—a wife is not much more than an ornament in her husband's house. However, such a nonproductive wife was not even a remote possibility for ordinary Nordic people in Ibsen's or any earlier time.

In the past, because of a stingy environment, Nordic people were not completely settled; they exploited distant resources, which meant that men were absent for extended periods fishing, hunting, trading, mining, soldiering, or working in the woods. And Nordic people were more dependent on livestock than on crops.

Livestock can be nurtured with the same knowledge and the same skill-set used to nurture young children—it was natural for women to be responsible for livestock, but because men were frequently absent, it was also a necessity. That made women responsible for home, family, and livestock (usually the principal source of food). Women's responsibilities were equal or more important than men's. In other societies these circumstances have led to a matriarchal society, and in the Nordic region it apparently led to independent women.[40]

Until the Viking era, there are no Nordic writings, and after the Viking era there are large gaps in Nordic written sources. Evidence must be taken from whatever sources are available, and some of these sources are not directly tied to Nordic people, including Herodotus.

Greek historian Herodotus (484–424 B.C.) recorded his observations in a book, *The Histories*. Likely the greatest Greek historian, his writing is today taken very seriously.[41] As with any writing, Herodotus must be examined critically, but he is a good source of information concerning the nomadic herders who lived north of the Black Sea. Herodotus visited this area himself and attempted to write about an earlier time (history), so his descriptions can be approximately dated to 550 B.C.

There is no proof that Herodotus' description of nomadic herders (Scythians, Sarmatians, and others) applies to ancient Nordic people, but there is evidence including, but not limited to, the fact that the name "Scythian" was replaced by the name "Goth," which applied generally to people in southern Scandinavia.[42]

There is historical and archeological evidence of repeated migrations of nomadic herders into western Europe. It is generally believed that one such migration carried a common language from India in the east to Europe in the west, the Indo-European language family including English. And there is DNA evidence of these migrations.[43] Herodotus' account of the attitude toward women is relevant:

> In other respects the Issedonians are reputed to be observers of justice: and it is remarked that their women have equal authority with the men.[44]

> The women of the Sauromatœ have continued from that day to the present to observe their ancient customs, frequently hunting on horseback with their husbands, sometimes even unaccompanied; in war taking the field [warriors]; and wearing the very same dress as the men.[45]

Herodotus referred to specific tribes of nomadic herders, Issedonians and Sauromatæ, but archeological and literary evidence indicates that these quotes apply to other herders including Scythians.[46] Immigrants carry their culture with them when they immigrate, which, in this case included "equal authority" for women.

About twenty-one centuries ago, ancient Nordic people began migrating south across Europe where they eventually came into contact with, and conflict with, Romans.[47] In A.D. 98, Roman historian Tacitus wrote a detailed account of these ancient Nordic people whom he labeled "Germanic."[48] All writings should be read critically including Tacitus, but he is, reportedly, the best Roman historian. Like all writers, he was affected by his own values, and he has been accused of preaching to his Roman audience. Tacitus is widely regarded as an excellent source, and there is little difficulty in making a Nordic connection:

> We now meet the Germanic people under their correct name and we get a fascinating insight into our own [Nordic] prehistory as it relates to customs, philosophy and political conditions. . . . Our knowledge comes principally . . . from the enlightening description of Tacitus.[49]
>
> —*Göran Burenhult*

Danish, Icelandic, Norwegian, and Swedish (and English) are Germanic languages but Finnish is not. The Karelian people of eastern Finland reportedly had extended families, and from that we might guess that Karelian women did not share the same status as other Nordic women.[50] Elsewhere in Finland there was a long history of interaction between the Finns and other Nordic people, and the Nordic attitude described in these pages applies equally well to Finns as it does to other Nordic people, regardless of language.[51]

Ancient Nordic people in Tacitus' time lived principally in southwestern Finland including the coastal area to the north, southern Sweden and a coastal area farther north, Oslo fjord and Trondheim fjord districts, all of the coastal areas of Norway, and Denmark. Iceland was not settled. Large northern as well as interior areas of Finland, Norway, and Sweden were sparsely occupied by Sami people or their ancestors.[52]

Almost two millennia ago, Tacitus described ancient Nordic attitude toward women:

> [Men] even believe that the sex [women] has a certain sanctity and prescience, and they do not despise their counsels, or make light of their answers.[53]

> [The woman] is reminded by the ceremony which inaugurates marriage that she is her husband's partner in toil and danger.[54]

In these quotes, Tacitus may have been scoffing at Nordic men because a Roman man would not listen to, or take seriously, the counsel of his wife. She was, at best, his servant. It has even been suggested that seating for free women at the Roman Coliseum was inferior to the seating for slaves.

Comparing Herodotus and Tacitus, side by side, it appears as if they were describing the same people:

550 B.C., women: hunting on horseback ... taking the field [warriors]

A.D. 98, women: suffer and dare ... in war ... [receive] steed, the gift of arms

550 B.C., women: have equal authority with the men

A.D. 98, women: management of ... home ... land ... husband's partner

Ancient Greece and Rome were the fountainheads of democracy, culture, and knowledge, whereas the nomadic herders described by Herodotus and the Germanic people described by Tacitus were rude barbarians. That is a myth, a myth that shrouds—even today—Herodotus' and Tacitus' comments relating to ancient Nordic culture. Because of that myth, ancient Nordic culture is nearly invisible.[55] Invisible or not, Herodotus' writing is useful evidence of ancient Nordic culture 2500 years ago, and Tacitus' writing is accepted evidence of ancient Nordic culture 1900 years ago.

Visigoths (west-Goths) and Ostrogoths (east-Goths) were Nordic descendants who overran the Roman Empire during the so-called Folk-Wandering era (A.D. 400–650). A tale from early in this period, *Völsunga Saga,* told of a warrior maiden, Brynhild, who taught great wisdom (a code of ethics) to the hero Sigurd (*Siegfried*). Considerable evidence has survived that this tale was popular in the Nordic region where—apparently—it was reasonable for a woman to be the keeper of great wisdom.[56]

[Viking] wives were certainly skilled and independent women . . . when their husbands were gone trading or on other trips they had to take responsibility for everything, both in the home and outside.[57]

—Astrid Gustafsson

From seven to ten centuries after Tacitus, in the Viking era, there is abundant evidence of Nordic culture. Women are not only mentioned frequently in the Icelandic sagas, but in stories such as *Laxdæla Saga,* women play key roles (more interesting roles than men).[58] In these sagas, consistent with what Tacitus reported nine hundred years earlier, a Nordic wife was a "partner" in marriage, and she could leave a marriage as easily as her husband.[59]

Combining information from archeology, rune stones, ancient laws, and contemporary writings including the Icelandic sagas, a present-day Swedish authority wrote:

Free women had a surprisingly strong position in society. . . . the free woman was an equal partner to her husband, but that did not mean that she was equal. . . . [For example,] a woman needed her husband's permission for economic transaction, or her father's if she was unmarried. . . . That compares with today in certain southern European countries where women continue to need their husband's permission to withdraw money from a bank or make a loan. . . . In politics and at the *ting* [democratic assembly] women played a less important role [than men] even if

25

women farm owners had a right to participate at
the *ting*. . . . For their time, the Nordic woman's
position was very strong. . . . Foreign merchants
were bug-eyed when they saw Viking women
who were craftsmen, landowners, and . . .[60]

—Catharina Ingelman-Sundberg

A noted social historian of the early twentieth century
described a different attitude toward women in feudal era
Germany than elsewhere in Europe. Here, among Germanic
people, naming practices indicate that the mother's family
was almost as important as the father's family. Among
other Europeans, a wife only partly (and not necessarily
permanently) belonged to what was, essentially, her
husband's family.[61]

Otherwise, in central Europe and Russia one thousand
years ago, patriarchal extended families were the norm,
and everyone (male and female) was subject to a family
patriarch (usually the oldest male).[62] In addition, everyone
was subject to a landlord or other aristocrat, as well as
some type of prince. Patriarchs had considerable sway,
but otherwise ordinary people (men and women) were
dependent, subjugated. And a wife's status was inferior to
that of her subjugated husband in most of Europe.

Changing economic conditions had a long-term
negative effect on the traditional Nordic attitude toward
women. Economics played its role most effectively in the
same areas where an aristocracy developed, usually where
there was significant areas of good cropland. Here, people
became more settled, more dependent on crops, and more
controlled by aristocratic landowners. Both men and women

were less independent in these areas, and this was evident in courtship and marriage traditions.

The adoption of Christianity excluded women from participating in their own religion. Christianity may have originally had a strong appeal for Nordic women, but once established it was a negative influence.[63] Four hundred years ago, a thoughtful philosopher wrote:

> The wife extends to her husband obedience, subjection, trust, compliance, services, support, aid, honor, reverence, modesty, and respect. . . without his council and consent she does nothing.[64]
>
> —*Johannes Althusius*

This quote sums up a Lutheran clergyman's positive attitude toward women in 1600. On the negative side, original sin, women's sins, and many of men's sins were all attributed to women.[65]

Severe laws regulating sexual activity in the centuries after A.D. 1500 have led some authorities to conclude that religion played a strong role in the Nordic area. Such laws were enforced among the Pilgrims in Massachusetts where sex before marriage, or even for a married couple on Sunday, was illegal.

Such laws may have been enforced in central and southern Europe, but they probably were not effective in the Nordic area.[66] For example, during the Catholic period, it was common for Nordic priests, even bishops, to be married and/or to have concubines.[67] This was absolutely against the teaching of the Church, but most Nordic clergy ignored that teaching.

27

In the Nordic area, religion was usually separate, and it did not regulate everyday life as it did elsewhere. Frequently, women made as great or a greater economic contribution than men while men were often absent. Because of their economic role and because, here, practicality trumped religion, Nordic marriage and courtship practices did not generally follow church doctrine.[68]

> [Early 1800s Norway, Hans Nielsen Hauge] allowed women to preach publicly, and to be in charge of "friendship groups."[69]
>
> —*Eva Maagerø, Birte Simonsen*

For poorer (the most equal) Nordic people, a reduced status for women may have been only skin-deep. Among Nordic religious dissidents in the 1800s, women sometimes conducted meetings or preached, and they were respected teachers.[70] Women were supposed to remain silent in State Churches, but it didn't go much further than that:

> During Easter 1850 . . . one evening at the school house, [Pastor] Wiberg read one of Luther's sermons. One of these women who usually would start the arguments, heard Wiberg say "You women remain silent in the gathering." and she answered "No way, not outside the church walls!"[71]

The legal and political rights of Nordic women is a subject that could fill volumes. Here, we will be satisfied with general trends illustrated by a few specifics. In the Viking era, Nordic women were not legally equal; democratic assemblies (*ting*) were composed of landowners, and only an occasional woman (a widow) owned land. But, where a woman owned land, she could participate in a *ting*, both one thousand years ago as well as centuries later. During the 1500s non-landowners participated in democratic assemblies, and some of them were women.[72] In the 1700s, landowning Nordic women in Sweden voted in local elections; they were still not equal, but neither were they excluded.[73]

The right to vote is an oft-cited barometer of progress for women. New Zealand women voted in 1893; Colorado women voted in 1897; Australian women voted in 1902; women voted in twelve American states west of the Mississippi by 1914. Women were in short supply in frontier areas and, perhaps, the right to vote was used as bait to attract them.

Finland and Norway were not frontiers. In 1906 women in Finland were granted full political equality—the first in the world—and in 1907, nineteen women were elected to the Finnish parliament—13 percent of the legislators.[74] Norwegian women were eligible to be elected in 1907 and received the right to vote in 1913.[75] The first woman (from Montana) joined the U.S. House of Representatives in 1917; women first voted in the U.S. presidential election of 1920. A woman first held national office in New Zealand in 1933, and the first Australian woman was elected to national office in 1943.

In the [Danish] coastal areas the farmer was often a fisherman as well, here and there a seaman, sailing far afield and for long periods leaving the working of his farm property to his wife.[76]

—*Peter Michelsen, Holger Rasmussen*

29

In the past, it was normal and natural for Nordic women to be independent, and this attitude could have been the offspring of a stingy environment and a dependence on livestock. Where it was necessary to exploit distant resources (timber, mining, fishing, hunting, trade, soldiering, jobs), men and women were often separated for significant periods. While men were gone women were responsible for everything—their economic role was at least equal to men. Anthropologist Kaj Birket-Smith said it best:

> [Because of] her importance in the struggle for sustenance . . . [a woman] often occupies a position which is actually, though not formally, equal to man's.[77]

Today, Nordic countries are competing with each other in a race for gender equality. On the World Economic Forum's "Gender Gap Report 2011," out of 135 countries, Iceland ranks #1, Norway ranks #2, Finland ranks #3, Sweden ranks #4, and Denmark ranks #6.

There is little controversy about the Nordic attitude toward women, in the past or today, but there are questions as to how this value affected other values. Did independent women influence family structure (nuclear versus extended)? If men cooperated with women regarding home and family, would that have made it easier for men to cooperate with others outside the home?

If both women and men influenced decision making, how did that affect culture? Research indicates that, compared to men, women are more averse to conflict, more apt to cooperate and work for consensus, more hardwired for empathy, more verbal, and more quick to innovate.[78]

Women did significantly impact Nordic culture; the question is how and to what degree.

The impact of women on culture (society) was a noteworthy part of a 1980 study by Dutch engineer and psychologist Geert Hofstede who ranked different societies on a masculine/feminine scale.[79] Among the most masculine societies were Japan with a score of 95 and the United States with a score of 62. Among the most feminine societies were Denmark (16), Norway (8), and Sweden (5). Nordic culture is different (the subject of this book), and no doubt women have played a much more significant role in the Nordic region than elsewhere, but the use of *masculine* and *feminine* could be misleading.

The meaning of these terms is culturally derived, as we have specific ideas about what it is to be "feminine" and what it is to be "masculine"; for example, some readers might equate "feminine" with a person who is soft, delicate, weak, and gentle. This definition might be appropriate for some women (or men) at some time, but our gender assumptions have changed over time; they are not the same as our parents', and not the same as our grandparents'. And different societies have different gender assumptions (what is expected of a female or of a male).

Today, Americans take for granted that women serve in the military, but that was not acceptable for earlier generations. And even now our American attitude is not identical to other societies.

In the Red Army, women were considered to be excellent soldiers, equal or superior to men.[80]

—*Elizabeth R. Skoglund*

31

During World War II at Stalingrad, the Red Army used snipers as one weapon in their epic battle against the Germans. Possibly the best-known of these snipers was a young woman who—one at a time—killed more than forty German soldiers (she referred to them as "sticks") before her career was cut short by an explosion. Was this young Russian sniper soft, delicate, weak, and gentle? No doubt her fiancé thought she was feminine.

And, if their young are threatened, human mothers have similar maternal instincts to those of other mammals. If you found yourself between a mother grizzly bear and her cubs, she might not seem soft, delicate, weak, and gentle.

"Masculine" and "feminine" have culturally derived meanings, different in different cultures; these words have no universal interpretation, but to the extent that Nordic culture is more cooperative, more adverse to conflict, has more empathy, attempts to resolve issues through dialogue, and is more innovative, it would be natural to suspect that women's role in society is the culprit.

A Long-Term Nordic Value: It is natural for women to be independent.

4

Independent Children

We were taught as children to be very dependent upon ourselves, not to ask for anything.[81]

—*Elsie Odmark*

This subject is routinely discussed from the perspective
of family structure: nuclear versus patriarchal extended
families. In these pages it is assumed that nuclear families,
which are ancient history in the Nordic region, equate
with independent children. Here, in the past, except for a
daughter who cared for her infirm parents, and except for
the son who was to inherit the land, children left home at
an early age and were then responsible for themselves—
they were independent. Elsewhere in Europe, in the past
paternalistic extended families were the rule. Adult siblings
and their children lived together—as extended families—
and they were subject to an older (usually the oldest) male
relative. Adult children were obligated to, and loyal to, the
patriarch—they were dependent.

But, in the Icelandic sagas and other literature we find exceptions: there were some Nordic extended families.[82] Some of the Nordic extended families mentioned in literature may have been upper class, but whether that is true or not, Nordic extended families were an exception among ordinary people. Nuclear families were the rule.[83]

And there were nuclear families in Europe outside of the Nordic region.[84] In spite of exceptions, patriarchal extended families were common in France up to the time of the Revolution, and these families were the rule in Russia into the twentieth century. The past is the foundation of the present, and in the past, generally, children elsewhere in Europe remained dependent even after they married and had children of their own, whereas Nordic children were on their own at an early age.[85] After they left home, children were not normally obligated to their family: they were responsible for themselves.

Nineteen hundred years ago, Roman historian Tacitus described ancient Nordic families:

> They live scattered and apart . . . every person surrounds his dwelling with an open space . . . [a wife is her husband's partner in toil and danger . . . each mother suckles her own offspring, and never entrusts it to servants and nurses . . . The young men marry late . . . Nor are the maidens hurried into marriage; the same age and a similar stature is required . . .[86]

Tacitus described nuclear families where children could not marry until they had established themselves. In extended families children could marry younger, and if a wife was subject to her husband, she might be much younger than he.

About four centuries after Tacitus, the Nordic value of being independent is evident in the Visigoth (west-Goth) law from Spain: "the free man must always retain control of his person." This Visigoth attitude was a direct contradiction of the prevailing attitude in southern Europe where men pledged a lifetime of service to their feudal lords.[87]

Seven hundred years after Tacitus, at the beginning of the Viking era, Nordic attitude was little changed: children were still expected to make their own way at a young age.[88] Each person was responsible for his or her own life.[89] A Viking might attach himself to a ship owner, but he could (and sometimes did) leave when it suited him. Vikings valued self-assertion.[90]

But, occasionally a scholarly text about the Vikings (or medieval Scandinavia) will be sprinkled with words and concepts borrowed from feudal Europe. For example, one authority states that there was loyalty between Viking men and their lord.[91] *Loyalty* and *lord* are words often associated with feudalism. In feudal Europe, men knelt, recited an oath, and pledged lifelong loyalty to their lord (they belonged to him). The use of these words might simply be an unfortunate translation, but there are other explanations.

The Icelandic sagas, the source for much information on the Vikings, were recorded some four centuries after the beginning of the Viking era. Christianity was then well established in Iceland; occasionally, that might have "colored" the sagas. For example, the earth-mother, Nerthus, becomes a male god, Njorth, in *Ynglings saga*.[92] Feudalism sometimes shadowed Catholicism as the religion migrated north from southern Europe; some feudal relationships existed in Iceland at the time the sagas were recorded and continuing up to the Reformation, but they were a minor exception in Nordic society.[93] Whatever the circumstances, the use of words or concepts borrowed from feudal Europe to describe Nordic people during the Viking era, or any other era, is misleading.

Feudal society was ruled by personal relationships, so-called "patron–client" relationships, while Viking society was ruled (however imperfectly) by laws.[94] In feudal society the group was the unit (not the individual) and men pledged lifetime loyalty to their lord. In Viking society the individual was the unit and men did not pledge lifelong loyalty to anyone.[95]

Nordic women and men in Viking and other times recognized mutual responsibilities; they thought of themselves as members of a group. Vikings on an expedition depended on each other and came to each other's defense. Sometimes extended families lived in long houses. But Viking society did not resemble feudal society.[96] Women had the right to divorce and pick another man if they wished; they could be involved in trade and sometimes owned land.[97] Both men and women were, first and foremost, independent individuals.[98] And Viking children were expected to be responsible for themselves at an early age.

Two centuries after the official Viking era, a Norwegian book, *The King's Mirror*, described—in detail—some values including:

> If children be given to you, let them not grow up
> without learning a trade; for we may expect a

man to keep closer to knowledge and business when he comes of age, if he is trained in youth while under control.[99]

This quote relates to education of children, but the author says "in youth while under control." In other words, if one was no longer a "youth," then one was no longer "under control." That Nordic children during the emigration era were independent at an early age, responsible for themselves, can be documented in books such as *Defiant Sisters* by Varpu Lindström, *I Go to America* by Joy Lintelman, and *New Land, New Lives* by Janet Rasmussen. *New Land, New Lives* contains numerous interviews with immigrants who relate how they were on their own—responsible for themselves— often after confirmation, about age fifteen.[100]

Examples from the Viking era, the Folk-Wandering era, the mid-1200s, and the early twentieth century suggest that there was apparent long-term continuity; Nordic children who weren't needed at home became responsible for themselves while they were teenagers, sometimes in their early teens. They were independent. That was not true in southern Europe and Russia.

Russian peasants, from the Viking era to the early twentieth century, had patriarchal extended families. Children were subject to their father, women were subject to their husbands, and both groups were subject to the family patriarch. Everyone was subject to the landlord or some prince, and everyone was subject to the absolute authority of the czar. Children were dependent and remained that way. Even the few young men who went to the city for work, did so as a collective—they were not on their own.[101] Finally, for hundreds of years, one half of all Russians were owned by someone—they could be mortgaged or sold.

In southern Europe there were more exceptions than in Russia (including areas that successfully resisted feudalism), but they *were* exceptions. Here, during the feudal era, up until the time of the French Revolution the "individual and the group appear inseparable."[102] The individual counted for little, the group (usually an extended family) was the unit, and everyone was subject to a master, their landlord. Ordinary people were only significant as part of a group, and they were subjugated, dependent. Here, as in Russia, dependent children grew up and became dependent adults.

Is there a connection between independent women and independent children? It seems self-apparent that a woman would be more independent in a nuclear family than in a patriarchal extended family. Author Varpu Lindström mentioned this in her book *Defiant Sisters*; in the extended families of the Karelians, young women were not expected to leave home and support themselves as was so among other Finns.[103]

Keeping children at home might increase the influence of a patriarch (empire building), but grown children living at home might make a woman's work more difficult.

One of the values measured in the *Human Beliefs and Values* surveys is whether parents must be respected even if they don't deserve it. Answering "no," the rankings were (out of seventy-eight countries): (1) Netherlands, (2) Sweden, (3) Norway, (4) Germany, (6) Iceland, (7) New Zealand, (8) Finland, and (24) United States.[104] Americans differed significantly on this question with more than twice as many people answering yes as was true for the Netherlands.

At this point, a reader might be wondering if independent children are really desirable. For example, who would care for old people? Sometimes a daughter stayed home and cared for parents who needed help. Sometimes the son who inherited land also inherited the obligation to keep his parents. But, if caring for old people was the only consideration, aged parents might have had a better safety net in an extended family.

Is it cruel to send children out on their own at age fifteen? "Maturity" is relative; circumstances may or may not require children to take on adult responsibilities. How about children sent out to "wander" who were expected to do whatever jobs they could find for something to eat?[105] This could easily be viewed as cruelty but if starvation was the alternative (during periodic famines, people did starve to death), then it was not cruel.

These "wander" children and the many Nordic children who left home at about age fifteen under more normal circumstances were all "on their own." They were responsible for themselves. That was not the case with English children during the Industrial Revolution. It was common to send English children as young as five away to work in factories, but these children were not independent. Presumably, it was in the factory owner's interest to act as a surrogate parent and take responsibility for the children.

Which is more modern, the patriarchal extended family that was long common in much of Europe, or the nuclear family that was common in the Nordic area? If you as a reader could choose for yourself, would you choose to make your own way at age fifteen or would you rather be dependent for your whole life?

Why is it significant that children were independent at an early age? Probably it strongly influenced Nordic attitude in three areas: education, equality, and importance of laws and institutions. In a stratified society (feudal, patriarchal extended families) people were ruled from above and they made few decisions for themselves. Laws and institutions were mostly window dressing—they were imposed from above; they were tools for controlling ordinary people. But in a society of independent individuals, laws and institutions (*ting*, laws, juries, etc.) came from the individuals themselves, and served as a mechanism for people to peacefully resolve their inevitable conflicts.[106] Laws are much more important for a group of detached individuals than they would be if one was a member of a family hierarchy or a stratified society.

Equality apparently was encouraged because children were raised by parents who were partners, and they were raised knowing that soon they would be independent of (detached from) their family. This must have changed a person's attitude toward others. When a fifteen-year-old (as she had long expected to do) left home, she essentially became an "other." [107] This could help explain the apparent contradiction, noted elsewhere, that Nordic people were independent individuals with a strong group identity.

Education was affected by children becoming independent at an early age; that is the next chapter.

A Long-term Nordic Value: It is natural for children to be responsible for themselves— independent—at an early age.

5

Education

[1930 in Finland] Only five per cent have an education beyond the elementary public schools, but only one per cent are illiterate. . . . Every home has good books; even factory girls are voracious readers of things worth reading. There is a library in every town . . .[108]

—Harry A. Franck

How do independent children relate to the success of societies or nations? If children were to become independent at an early age, before they left home they needed to have all the knowledge and skills they would require to survive (in a stingy environment).[109] By contrast, children raised in a paternalistic extended family did not require much education. They would not be responsible for themselves, they could be taught a few skills at a later date, and they were subject to a landlord and a prince who would not benefit from their education.

Thus, Nordic children would become responsible for themselves at an early age and their parents were responsible for teaching them everything they needed to know. As late as the mid-1800s this included many skills (weaving, knitting, sewing, baking, woodworking, ironworking, healing, and so on), but this chapter is focused on reading, writing, and arithmetic.

[Ca 1520] You parents cannot prepare a more dependable treasure for your children than an education in the liberal arts.

—*Martin Luther*

One thousand years ago, and long before that, Nordic people used the runic alphabet. The fact that they did not use the Roman alphabet is not an indication that they were backward. Americans do not use Roman numerals, and we do not speak the Roman language (Latin), but we are not backward. Some languages, including Latin, and some alphabets, including runes, died out. That does not prove that Latin was backward, or runes either.

The first literary mention of runes is in *Ynglings saga* where the god Odin uses runes that are associated with magic.[110] *Ynglings saga* was dated to about 100 B.C. by Swedish historian Anders Fryxell and, coincidentally, the first known runic inscription is from the same period.[111] There is insufficient evidence from this time period to say anything, except that Nordic ("Germanic") people were writing and reading runes two thousand years ago.

From the beginning of the Viking era (A.D. 800) until about A.D. 1600, runes were commonly used for the same reasons that we use writing today.[112] Runes were constructed of straight lines that were easy to carve in wood, but wood rots and wood burns; with few exceptions, rune writing on wood was lost. But runes were also used for memorial stones; many of these were broken up or used for other purposes, but they did not rot or burn, and thousands of them survived. These rune stones are silent witnesses that Nordic people wrote and read runes more than a thousand years ago.

Eight hundred years ago a big change was underway in the Nordic region: in several locations people were using the Roman alphabet to write on paper or vellum. Works such as the Icelandic sagas and the Norwegian law code were written in the vernacular, the spoken language of local people—they were written to be read by ordinary people.

The King's Mirror was also written at this time in the vernacular (Old Norse); it is an amazing source of information about the Nordic attitude toward education:

> . . . whenever you have an hour to spare you should give thought to your studies, especially to the law books; for it is clear that those who gain knowledge from books have keener wits than others . . . Make a study of all the laws, but while you remain a merchant there is no law that you will need to know more thoroughly than the Bjarkey [Birka] code . . . But although I have most to say about laws, I regard no man perfect in knowledge unless he has thoroughly learned and mastered the customs of the place where he is sojourning. And if you wish to become perfect

in knowledge, you must learn all the languages, first of all Latin and French [the official language in contemporary England], for these idioms are most widely used; and yet, do not neglect your native tongue or speech. . . . Learn arithmetic thoroughly, for merchants have a great need for that.[113]

The King's Mirror was written by an upper-class man as advice to a young man who would be involved in trade—a merchant (imagine a Christian Viking trader). Nonetheless, the strong emphasis on education evident in this quote applied to ordinary people. For example, there is evidence from this period that it was not unheard of for an ordinary Nordic man, a farmer, to be so well-informed that he could debate fine points of the law.[114]

Most ordinary people did not need to learn Latin or French, but they needed to be educated, and much of that education needed to be acquired before they left home: not just skills, reading, and writing, but also arithmetic (as mentioned in the last quote). Navigation sometimes required arithmetic, as did buying and selling at markets, and figuring how much seed was required for a field or how many cows could be over-wintered with the feed that had been stored away. Nordic people were responsible for themselves; they made their own decisions; they needed arithmetic.

Evidence of literacy at the time of *The Kings Mirror* was a side-benefit of a fire in Bergen, Norway, on July 4, 1955. A block of historic buildings on the waterfront were destroyed, and an insightful archeologist recognized this as an opportunity. An archeological dig in the soil beneath the destroyed buildings uncovered over six hundred wooden objects with runic inscriptions; they had been preserved because they were sealed in mud. These inscriptions were business agreements, personal letters, scribbling, love messages, etc. dating to the 1200s and 1300s. They are strong evidence that ordinary Nordic people in Bergen were literate in the 1200s and 1300s.[115]

> [In Novgorod] scraps of birch-bark were used for shopping lists, for indicating the contents of vessels and their quality, for scrawling out promissory notes. Literacy was widespread; in fact, in Novgorod there existed some sort of birch-bark writing school, evidence of which we find in sheets of birch-bark bearing alphabetical exercises written in a child's hand . . .[116]
>
> —*Asko Vilkuna*

While people carved messages in wood in Bergen, people in Novgorod carved messages in birch bark. Two centuries earlier, Novgorod had been a Viking trade center, and in the 1200s and 1300s it was located in a Finnish district of Russia (about 260 miles southeast of present-day Helsinki). Here, 780 birch bark scrolls were unearthed, preserved in the same way as the Bergen wooden objects, sealed in mud. The scroll messages (written in the Russian alphabet) were personal letters, obituaries, dun letters, shopping lists, alphabetical exercises, charms, agreements, and so on. One message used Finnish names, and another was written in the Finnish language (circa early thirteenth century). At this time, in the ancient Viking trade center of Novgorod, "Literacy was widespread . . ."[117] "Both men and women wrote."[118]

The preceding paragraphs document evidence of pre-Reformation Nordic literacy. A possible conclusion from the evidence is that elsewhere in Europe it was not unusual for the upper class to be illiterate, but in the Nordic area it was common for ordinary people to be literate.[119]

[1904] With regard to the *Dissemination of Knowledge among the People* it will probably be a well-known fact that the Scandinavian nations occupy a very prominent position.[120]

—*Gustav Sundbärg*

On October 31, 1517, Martin Luther nailed his ninety-five theses on the castle church at Wittenberg, Germany. During the following century, under varying circumstances, the Nordic countries changed from Catholic to Lutheran and established State Churches. Luther believed that ordinary people should read the Bible and children should be educated. This thought was echoed at the beginning of the 1600s:

For parents should educate their children.

—*Johannes Althusius*

Althusius was a prominent German clergyman who was quoted earlier for his traditional (southern European) attitude toward women; nonetheless, his attitude toward education was modern, and he will be quoted later because of his futuristic (or ancient) attitude toward political authority.

If I could leave [preaching] . . . there is no office I would rather have than that of schoolmaster or teacher.

—Martin Luther

At this time, the early 1600s, Nordic State Churches began insisting that all children learn to read the Catechism. Probably, because of the State Church demands, reading books for children were printed in several locations. In Stockholm in 1611, an ABC book was published showing both runes and the then-new Gothic letters. This could be interpreted to mean that people were still using runes and that it would help them to learn the new alphabet if they saw runes and Roman letters next to each other.[121] Decades earlier in 1543, a book to help children learn the Catechism, *Abckiria,* was published in Finland.[122]

Children's reading books were published in many locations including America for children of Scandinavian immigrants. The page below is from a book published in Illinois; it illustrates how children were taught to count— they also needed to learn arithmetic.[123]

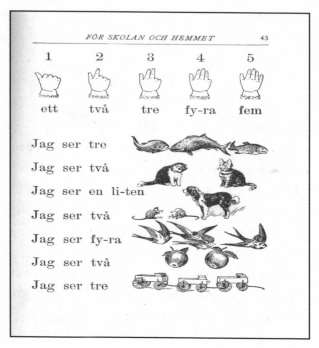

FÖR SKOLAN OCH HEMMET 43

1	2	3	4	5
ett	två	tre	fy-ra	fem

Jag ser tre

Jag ser två

Jag ser en li-ten

Jag ser två

Jag ser fy-ra

Jag ser två

Jag ser tre

This page illustrates something else: it was meant for "*Skolan och Hemmet*,"—to be used in the school and the home. In much of the Nordic area up to the mid-1800s, children were taught in homes by a mother or another adult. Obviously these adults (women and men) were literate or they could not have been teachers. But sometimes, perhaps often, children taught children. If you have ever had an opportunity to attend a one-room school, you probably witnessed children teaching other children, but this also happened at home. A Canadian traveling in Saskatchewan in 1895–1896 witnessed a six-year-old girl (the daughter of Finnish immigrants) teaching her sister—less than five years old—to read the Catechism.[124] Teaching children in homes was the rule in the Nordic area for centuries, except in Denmark and Norway.

Royal (government) schools were established in Denmark starting in the 1620s, but in the mainland part of Denmark, Jutland, some "peasant-schools" already existed and continued for a time in competition with the new government schools. In Norway because there were few cities, "school" often consisted of a circuit-riding teacher.[125]

State Church demands that everyone read and understand the Catechism resulted in universal literacy, but—probably—the State Churches did not need to persuade Nordic parents of the value of education.[126] It is reasonable to speculate that the quotes above from Martin Luther and Johannes Althusius represented long-held beliefs in the north—parents were responsible for educating their children.

In the 1680s, a pastor in Vonsild Parish of Denmark was in the habit of writing a brief obituary for people when he recorded their death in the church book. But a young woman's death in 1688 was so dramatic that the pastor was inspired to write a longer obituary including this passage:

Mette Jensdatter was a servant girl, often unemployed during the winter months, who had taught herself to read. She was self-taught and enjoyed reading. After becoming aware of a new, inexpensive Danish history book, she borrowed enough money, walked some distance to a market town, and purchased the book. On the way home she became lost in a late season snowstorm and perished. She was found in the snow with her book.[127]

About 530 miles northeast of Vonsild Parish and one-and-a-half centuries after Mette Jensdatter, Per Andersson was born in the early 1800s and raised in a small forest community, four hours' walking distance from church or village. He and his family were backwoods folk (forest farmers). According to his son, Daniel, Per had not a single day of formal schooling and yet he was an accomplished writer.[128] Here is a translated excerpt from a letter that Per wrote in 1852 to his friend Eric Norelius, founder of Gustavus Adolphus College in Minnesota:

> I have now had letters from Sweden, which you said were on the way. There is nothing remarkable in them or about anyone but only complaints about poor crops and hard times, lack of money, and severe winter weather and a cold spring so they could drive on Hassela Lake in the beginning of May. And that many want to come here, but . . .[129]

—Emory Johnson, translator

It would be natural to speculate about how typical Mette Jensdatter and Per Andersson were for their times. But, we don't need to speculate about literacy in the Nordic countries. Egil Johansson of Sweden ("The History of Literacy in Sweden," etc.) and Charlotte Appel of Denmark (*Læsning og Bogmarked I 1600-tallets Danmark*) have extensively researched literacy in the Nordic area. Johansson's work applies generally to Sweden, Finland, and Iceland while Appel's work applies generally to Denmark and Norway. Appel's book contains some information on Johansson's work (pages 59–65), and she has a fifty-page summary in English.

Because of the research of Johansson and Appel, we can say with some certainty that by 1740, 90 percent of Nordic men and women were "literate" (they could read a book), many of them could write, and (along with reading and writing) many of them had been exposed to arithmetic.[130] Two centuries ago we have an excellent example of Nordic literacy: two hundred thousand copies of the writing of Hans Nielsen Hauge were printed and distributed in Norway, whose population, counting everyone, totaled nine hundred thousand. Hauge was a religious dissident, so presumably the State Church played no role in this.[131]

In her book *Defiant Sisters* historian and author Varpu Lindström wrote that when large numbers of schools were established in rural areas of Finland in the late 1800s, it was assumed that pupils for these schools had already learned to read—before they entered school.[132]

In other areas of Europe there were no rapid changes in literacy among ordinary people. In France feudalism lasted until the revolution in 1789, and in the early 1800s most Frenchmen were still illiterate.[133] In the early 1600s England had grammar schools, but they were "heavily socially restricted" (for the upper class).[134] England was the first country to industrialize (starting in the 1700s) and that is implicitly accepted as "progress." But one author has suggested that literacy in England declined after industrialization began.[135] That would not be surprising because children as young as five were sent away to work in factories—there was no time to teach them to read. Presumably, in the early 1800s most ordinary people in England were still illiterate. In Russia, feudalism was outlawed about 1850, but there was no significant change until the early twentieth-century revolution. Generally, except for soldiers, ordinary Russians were still illiterate in the mid-1800s.

The education of children may depend on the flow of "authority" in society. For example, there is evidence from feudal Russia that some ordinary people wanted to, and attempted to, educate their children. But there were restrictive regulations; neither the State nor the nobility would benefit from educating serfs. To whatever extent ordinary Russians wanted to educate their children, they were hindered not only by the government but by the upper class—the only push to educate ordinary children came from their parents.[136] Where authority flows from the top down (stratified societies), education is retarded. Where authority flows from the bottom up (equal societies), education is encouraged.

Nordic countries rank high on a variety of education indexes available on the Internet, but often they are not tightly grouped. Education indexes give the impression of significant differences among the Nordic countries. This may be partly true, but some of the differences may be due to the difficulty of measuring different educational systems, or to problems with the index itself. For example, a ranking of per capita engineering bachelor's degrees omits Denmark altogether. On the same index, Denmark ranks sixth in the world in engineering doctoral degrees.[137] This appears to be contradictory.

Again, on the World Health Organization's indexes of reading, math, and science scores for fifteen-year-olds, Nordic countries rank high, but they are not tightly grouped. A notable feature of these indexes is that there is only about 20 percent difference between the top-ranked country and the thirtieth-ranked country. It is reasonable to speculate here that the data for Nordic countries is very accurate, but the same thing may not be true for southern European and other countries that have a more relaxed attitude toward their data.[138]

In 2011 the Canadian Higher Education Strategy Associates ranked eighteen countries by the "affordability" and "accessibility" of higher education. Higher education was most affordable and accessible in: Finland (first and first), Norway (second and third), Germany (third and eleventh), Denmark (fourth and not rated), Sweden (fifth and ninth), Netherlands (sixth and second), France (seventh and tenth), and so on.

The literacy chart for military conscripts in Chapter One was accurate. Ordinary people in the Nordic countries (along with Germany, the Netherlands, and Switzerland) were more literate than other Europeans—they were more modern. [139]

Parents should provide children with, food, clothing, education, and a Christian upbringing.[140]

—*Danish folk saying circa A.D. 1600*

Today education is a top priority, and Nordic countries are world leaders in it.[141] This has not gone unnoticed, and has resulted in frequent visits to Nordic countries by foreign educators. For example, reportedly the Finns were at first amused when foreigners showed up to examine the Finnish education system, but eventually the amusement wore off when the foreign educators kept coming.

A Long-Term Nordic Value:
Children must be educated.

6

Equality

All Side by Side, High and Low, Educated and
Uneducated, Businessman and Worker.[142]

—Motto of mid-1800s' upper-class Nordic fraternal society,
Skarpskyttelägret

Nordic equality is not theologically based as in
Thomas Jefferson's "all men are created equal," and it is
not the idealistic "equality" of Enlightenment philosophers
mentioned in Chapter Ten; instead it is hardheaded
and practical. There are differences in status, there are
differences in wealth, but nevertheless—regardless of
wealth or status—everyone is equal. In the past, status was
"class," but today Nordic status is usually a by-product of
skill or achievement. And, as income differences become
greater, equality becomes less likely; if people are equal
there is an assumption that income inequality is not large
enough to interfere.[143]

In the summary of Chapter Four it was mentioned that
equality may have been encouraged because children were

not simply independent, they were detached from their family—they essentially became an "other." It would have been natural for them to identify with others—to value equality. They were independent but they recognized a shared self-interest and a shared humanity with others.

A French sociologist had a different perspective on this issue: political values mirror family structure (remember, independent children are a product of nuclear families). Emmanuel Todd wrote that the French Revolution and its motto "Liberty, Brotherhood, and Equality" originated in districts with nuclear families (Franks = Germanic influence).[144] But in areas of France with Celtic and Basque influence, where extended families predominated, the revolution and its slogan were not popular.[145] In other words, Todd believed that nuclear families (independent children) equate with equality.

In the distant past, Nordic equality was natural because of a lack of highly visible classes (most people lived and dressed the same); because upper class people used the same tools, depended on the same resources, and worked shoulder-to-shoulder with lower class people; and because of social mobility (upper-class individuals might be only one or two generations removed from the lower class).[146] Nordic people acted as if everyone were a full human being; they practiced what Thomas Jefferson preached in the Declaration of Independence: "all men are created equal."

After the Viking Era, an upper class gradually developed in some Nordic areas that lived differently than ordinary people and dressed differently than ordinary people. This upper class eventually became clearly visible and, imitating their contemporaries in central and southern Europe, they expected ordinary people to show physical signs of submission—deference. And, because it is accepted that Nordic people value equality, deference will be the single element of equality to be explored in detail.

Physical deference could be removing any head-covering, bowing one's head, bowing at the waist, bowing and scraping, or prostrating oneself at a high-status individual's feet. Verbal deference usually included a title (master, sir, my lord) together with words that showed humility.

Traditionally, Nordic people did not give or expect deference, while ordinary non-Nordic Europeans were required to reinforce their humble status by various forms of deference.[147] During the feudal era, the most noteworthy act of deference occurred when an ordinary man pledged his lifetime service and allegiance. In this feudal ceremony, he put his hands together, palm to palm, and placed them inside the hands of his master, at the same time uttering a short verbal deference including words such as "my lord." He was submitting to—humbling himself before—his lord.[148]

After the clasping of hands, the lifelong lord-underling contract was sealed by the men kissing on the lips. Not surprisingly, this ritual never took root in the Nordic region, and besides was rarely used elsewhere in Europe in any area influenced by Nordic culture.[149] But it was used when a Nordic leader, Rollo, became Duke of Normandy province in France about A.D. 911.

According to legend, during his coronation ceremony Rollo was asked to put his hands between the hands of the French king, which he did, but which "neither his father, nor his grandfather, nor his great-grandfather before him had ever done for any man." But when he was told to kneel and kiss the king's foot, he absolutely refused.[150] Instead, Rollo asked one of his men to do it, and he also refused at first, but then thought of a solution. Rollo's man grabbed the king's foot and raised it high enough so that the king fell over, causing much laughter. This tale, be it fact or fiction, demonstrates a factual difference in culture.[151]

Starting about eight hundred years ago, usually in areas with a significant amount of good cropland, an aristocracy sprouted in Denmark, southern Sweden, parts of Finland, and parts of Norway. Century after century this entitled upper class tirelessly promoted their self-interest. For our purposes it matters not whether this aristocracy was nobility or lesser nobility or something else. What matters is that they were politically entitled and economically capable of challenging equality. It was in their interest to be surrounded by humble peasants, and peasants in the rest of Europe humbled themselves to their aristocracy. Why shouldn't this be the case in the Nordic region? It was. In those areas where the aristocracy took root, ordinary Nordic people were required to exhibit both physical and verbal deference.

For example, most of the cropland in Denmark had long been controlled by its aristocracy when feudalism was legalized there in the 1700s. The period of nationwide feudalism was brief (thirty years ending in 1777) and it was mild feudalism; serfs could not be bought and sold. But most ordinary Danes had long been in daily contact with an aristocracy: they did what they had to do. They were, as occasion required, forced to show deference but they were not humble. As Nordic people always had, they thought of themselves as full human beings, and they did not look up to or admire the upper class.[152]

And the same attitude is true for the *statare* in Sweden. S*tatare*, usually married couples hired by the year for farm work, were at the bottom of society. Their lives during the 1930s were the subject of a novel, *En natt i juli*, by Jan Fridegård. The lower-class men and women of this novel did not look up to or admire their upper-class employer. In conversation, they spoke level, eye to eye, with him. When a sheriff visited a *statare* cottage, there was equal disrespect. The sheriff entered the cottage rudely; the *statare* husband made a veiled threat against the sheriff, while his wife cursed the sheriff as he left. These *statare* were not humble.

Fridegård's book about the *statare* is fiction, and readers may naturally question the use of fiction as evidence. But, for fiction to be read and appreciated, it must ring true for those reading it—it had to seem reasonable to its contemporary Swedish audience.[153] Fridegård was very familiar with his subject, and beyond that, evidence does not always come in a standard package. There is no single approved form for evidence.[154]

The aristocracy's centuries-long efforts to humble Nordic people were reinforced by Christianity. Christians were encouraged to be obedient and humble, to meekly accept suffering. This Christian attitude was the polar opposite of the traditional Nordic attitude that admired strength and individual initiative.[155] After a millennium of Christian teaching, even in areas with a long-established aristocracy, ordinary Nordic people could be forced to show deference, but they were not humble. To whatever extent Christianity taught humility, that teaching failed in the Nordic region.

The bönder [farmers] of Sweden have never been serfs or slaves. They have always been free men, very generally owners of the freehold of their farms, and by their courage and independence have made and unmade even the kings of the realm.[156]

—*W.W. Thomas, Jr.*

An aristocracy forced people to show deference, but most of the Nordic region had no aristocracy. People lived their lives with little or no contact with any aristocratic upper class; they neither expected nor showed deference.[157] When people met, when they talked, they were level—one person to another. Their attitude, a reluctance to show deference under any circumstances, has been labeled "vigorous self-assertion," being "defiant," "stubborn," or "stiff-necked."[158]

Often stiff-necked people lived right across a border from areas dominated by an aristocracy. For example, during the Middle Ages, Denmark with a long-established aristocracy bordered forested areas of Sweden that had no aristocracy. We may assume that equality next door made it more difficult for the aristocracy to maintain its aristocratic traditions including deference rituals. Possibly from the nineteenth century onward, physical and verbal deference in the Nordic region gradually diminished until sometime in the twentieth century when Nordic people attempted to eliminate all visible symbols of class.[159] The Nordic attitude toward deference had returned to that of its traditional roots, an attitude that was never abandoned in much of the Nordic area.

[1856, Sweden] A Dalecarlian always says "thou" to his pastor, which is like calling a man by his first name with us [Americans].[160]

—*Charles Loring Brace*

Eleven hundred years ago, Rollo and his Nordic warriors were reluctant to show deference. More than one thousand years later and far to the north, modern Nordic warriors apparently shared Rollo's attitude. These warriors, Finns who fought Russia between 1939 and 1944, were immortalized in *The Unknown Soldier* by Väinö Linna. Repeatedly in this novel, some of the best combat soldiers, if they were sitting and an officer approached, refused to stand; they refused to salute; they refused to show any deference to officers. These men were inadequately equipped, poorly fed, badly outnumbered, and yet they were tenacious and efficient soldiers—the best.[161]

[1865-67] The Russian peasants and native peasants whom we met removed their caps and held them respectfully in their hands while we [Americans] passed . . .[162]

—*George Keenan*

In central Europe and Russia roughly one thousand years ago, ordinary people accepted that their lives were ruled by others, and they accepted physical and verbal deference. They humbled themselves. Certainly there were many variations and exceptions: people sometimes revolted against unjust rulers, and not everyone was humble, but generally we may imagine that people accepted subjugation, so there would be no reason not to humble oneself.

What an aristocracy we have in England. Is there anything like it in the world? . . . They're jolly good chaps . . .[163]

—1930s, unemployed worker to Peter Freuchen

There must have been changes over time in deference rituals in Europe, variations by country or ruler, but the upper-class attitude toward ordinary people was unchallenged until the 1700s, and we may assume there was no real change in deference in central Europe and Russia except through bloody revolutions (1789 in France, 1918 in Russia).

What is so important about showing deference? Who cares if somebody bows, or if that person addresses another using a title? What's wrong with a little humility? Physical and verbal deference as it appears in English period novels and movies is similar to period costumes: innocent and charming—nothing more.

That is one way of looking at it, but not the only way. What if people *internalize* the constant humbling rituals and actually believe that they are inferior? If they believe they are inferior to the upper class, it would be natural to believe that the upper class should rule, should have a monopoly on political power. Something like that was true during the Middle Ages in central Europe where ordinary people accepted absolute rulers, or in Russia where ordinary people believed it was necessary to have absolute rulers. As far as period novels and movies are concerned, for ordinary Europeans, deference was the line separating those for whom opportunity came with birth from those for whom opportunity never came.

Physical and verbal deference were *visible* evidence of inequality (a stratified society). Nordic people were sometimes stiff-necked because they regarded both themselves and others as equals.

Because there is general agreement that the Nordic people value equality, this chapter has been limited to a few paragraphs relating to deference. Nonetheless, the significance of the Nordic equality cannot be overstressed. Equality applied regardless of wealth or status:

> [I]t pained him [upper class Norwegian arctic explorer Nansen] greatly to be the sole recipient of these distinctions. He felt strongly that his comrades [ordinary men] . . . ought also to share with him the public recognition of their exploit.[164]

This value is taught to children by parents and by other members of the community, and it is taught in schools. Students are taught to stand up for themselves, they are taught to stand up for what is right, and they are taught social awareness: to think about and respect others.[165] Children are taught to express their individuality in a way that does not harm others.

There is social pressure to not stand out from the group, to be a good equal member. Being reserved or reticent might have been encouraged by the realization that there was nothing to be gained by drawing attention to oneself; any sign of individual self-importance would meet quick resistance from others.[166] This value (all are equal, and no one should stand above or below the group) is reflected in terms such as *Janteloven, lagom,* and *moderasjo.*

Today, apparently many Nordic medical doctors, scientists, and university professors do not use their titles. Whatever its advantages, this social leveling is sometimes credited with producing low personal incentive; except for that possibility, equality apparently has a significant and healthy impact on disease, crime, politics, and more.[167]

A Long-term Nordic Value: Everyone,
regardless of wealth or status, is equal.

7

Group Identity
(Mutual Responsibilities)

Group identity is visible as mutual responsibilities; each individual owes to others (society), and expects from others (society), definite responsibilities. There is some overlap between mutual responsibilities and terms such as noncognitive skills, social capital, morals, character traits, ethical principles, and virtue; for example, honesty might play a role in all of these terms. But there are differences. Noncognitive skills are qualities such as persistence, dependability, and self-discipline that help an individual succeed. Social capital is values that help a society succeed (trust, reciprocity, etc.) including the radius (family, tribe, society) of those values. Morality, character, virtue, and ethics may be viewed as rules of conduct or values (what is expected of a good person): for example, courage, honesty, fairness, kindness, loyalty, and humility.

Society's attitude toward authority affects these values. Ethical principles, in a society that accepts top-down authority, might naturally include humility, obedience, and loyalty. A society with bottom-up authority would benefit if principles included empathy and modesty: here "empathy" is the ability to put oneself in someone else's shoes, and "modesty" means to avoid placing oneself above others. With bottom-up authority, natural principles include fairness and justice, respect, and cooperation.[168]

> The community which has neither poverty nor riches will always have the highest principles.
>
> —*Plato*

In much of central and southern Europe before the French Revolution (1789), and in Russia before the Russian Revolution (1918), feudalism and extended families were the rule. Society was highly stratified and authority came down from the top (including the Orthodox Church). Individuals' responsibilities to others included obedience to (higher) authority, loyalty to family, and communal work.

Rights and opportunities depended solely on personal connections, so-called "patron–client" relationships. Ordinary people were supposed to be loyal to, and obey, the family patriarch, the landlord, the local prince, the local priest, and the king or czar. Obedience, humility, and loyalty were responsibilities along with trying to be on the best possible terms with those in authority.

> Russia was not Sweden, where equivalent institutions were imbedded in political structure. In Russia . . . life chances were distributed through patron–client networks.[169]
>
> —*Geoffrey Hosking*

But, in feudal society, among ordinary people, there were no "individuals" as we are accustomed to thinking of that concept. Men were bound by kinship (family) and they pledged lifelong servitude to their "lord." The individual hardly existed except as a communal member of a group.[170] Individual responsibilities to others were nearly impossible. That society was the foundation for the present-era society in most of central and southern Europe as well as Russia.

"Group identity" in these pages may, in other publications, be referred to as: social cohesion, group solidarity, group-centered, unity, fellow-feeling, real humanity, communal, cooperative, bonds to society, and mutual sympathy.

> . . . fellow-feeling which . . . is a characteristic trait running through all classes of the [Swedish] community.[171]
>
> —*Gustav Sundbärg*

As with their European neighbors, Nordic people had a group identity, but not in the context of long-term feudalism; in the Nordic context, group identity went hand in hand with independent individuals and equality.

Group identity was most visible as responsibilities that each Nordic individual felt to others, including cooperation and consensus, justice and fairness, honesty and truth-telling, and respect.[172] These responsibilities are owed by the individual, not to any particular person, but to others generally—the group.

When asked if it is especially important to teach children a feeling of responsibility, Nordic people answered overwhelmingly yes: Norway 92 percent, Netherlands 87 percent, Sweden 87 percent, Finland 86 percent, Germany 84 percent, Italy 82 percent, Denmark 81 percent, Iceland 81 percent, Switzerland 80 percent, Canada 77 percent, Russia 76 percent, United States 72 percent, New Zealand 59 percent, and Great Britain 56 percent.[173]

When did mutual responsibilities originate? Per Albin Hansson, Swedish Prime Minister from 1932 to 1946, believed that desirable responsibilities in a family were also desirable responsibilities in a nation.[174] If it was desirable for a family to care for its own, and if the same was true for a community, why wouldn't it also be true for a nation? It was just a matter of extending the radius from family to nation. Dutch author Geert Hofstede (*Culture's Consequences*) theorized that the high status of women in Scandinavia influenced society there to be more cooperative, more prone to compromise.[175]

And there may be other theories, but here we will assume that mutual responsibilities are very old and that they are integral to Nordic culture. These responsibilities are being discussed as if they were separate values, but they might more correctly be viewed as various facets of a group identity.

Centuries ago, residents of Nordic villages cooperated with others and helped each other; culture included a strong aversion to asking for help, but when needed, it was there.

> Whenever a villager fell ill or suffered an accident, when he could not sow his field or do his haymaking in time, then his neighbors got together and did it for him—without compensation.[176]
>
> —*Vilhelm Moberg*

If you help someone who is sick or injured, knowing that others will help you if you are sick or injured, it is similar to insurance.

Cooperation was normal and natural. Men did fieldwork cooperatively and they hunted and fished as a group, cooperatively.[177] Local government and the *ting* were cooperative. English novelist H. Rider Haggard wrote in 1913:

> [W]isdom and brotherly understanding [of Danish farmers] . . . have enabled them to triumph over the difficulties of soil, climate, and low prices, and by the practice of general cooperation, to achieve individual and national success.[178]

Cooperation goes back to ancient times. Vikings cooperated on raid or trade expeditions. They were not communal; their ship was owned by one or more men, and each man received a share of the profits. However, they worked together—they were cooperating on a business venture. Cooperation continued to exist from ancient times into the present era. Even in Nordic areas that experienced feudalism, men still met and cooperated on planting, harvesting, and other decisions that affected the community.

But, cooperation is not separate: it is related to equality. A Viking ship owner did not have authority to conscript a crew for his ship. He had to attract individuals voluntarily, and they needed to act as a unit—cooperatively. In the 1800s, successive inheritances had divided farm land into small pieces, but people were equal—no one had authority to organize work. Fields could be efficiently planted and harvested only if everyone cooperated. Use of summer pastures, use of meadows for haying, use of the forests, and other activities were only efficient if they were done cooperatively.

Often these activities were facilitated by consensus (everyone agreed to cooperate). The men on a Viking ship, whether raiding or trading, were a unit (all for one and one for all). When participating in a *ting*, participants sometimes took an oath to support the community whatever was decided, and some decisions had to be unanimous.[179] Even where the only issue was setting a date for cooperative work, consensus was desirable—because of equality.

Nordic cooperation continued in the New World. Starting in the 1800s, English-Americans, German immigrants, and Scandinavian immigrants started various types of cooperative businesses. There were cooperative insurance companies, general stores, creameries, canneries, and other enterprises. But, the co-ops started by English-Americans and those started by German immigrants seldom lasted more than a year. Scandinavians were much more successful at running cooperative businesses because they were equals and they had an ancient tradition of cooperative decision making and cooperative work.[180]

Given the Nordic environment and given equality, cooperation was imperative, and often, consensus was necessary.

Trust is the foundation of human society, while lack of trust is its plague, and that trust is the bond of concord among the different members.[181]

—*Plato*

Honesty creates trust, which is a necessary ingredient for democracy, and which is the foundation of a healthy society and a healthy economy. It is a responsibility of each individual to be honest, but this responsibility is not to anyone in particular; it is to others generally—to the group. A Swedish-American wrote:

> The old [Nordic] culture brought about reverence for God and all things sacred, respect for law and order, honesty in word and deed, truthfulness.[182]

> —*Eric Norelius*

"Honesty" is generally passive (not lying or stealing), but "truthfulness" is active: it is speaking the truth even when that is unpleasant.[183] This, like cooperation, is an ancient Nordic tradition. Roman historian Tacitus wrote nineteen hundred years ago:

> [Ancient Nordic people are a] race without either natural or acquired cunning [deception]; they disclose their hidden thoughts.[184]

Apparently, Romans did not disclose their hidden thoughts; they did not speak truthfully.

"Audun's story" in the Icelandic sagas exemplifies truthfulness during the Viking era. Audun spent all of his money buying a polar bear as a gift for the Danish king. On his way to deliver this gift, Audun became dependent on the hospitality of Norwegian king Harald, who was at war with the Danish king. King Harald asked to purchase the bear, and Audun answered *truthfully* that he would not sell it because he was bringing it as a gift to the Danish king. King Harald could simply have killed Audun and taken the bear, but instead, he allowed Audun to continue on his journey. Audun's truthfulness, however offensive it was to King Harald, was not punished.[185]

A visitor about 1850 experienced Norwegian honesty:

An English gentleman, a year or two ago, traveling between Trondhjem and Christiania [Oslo], tied . . . [his satchel to the back of a carriage and thus] lost out fourteen or fifteen sovereigns. He wrote on arrival in Christiania, to the county judges, and in a few days had every one of the sovereigns returned to him. They had been picked up by the peasants, and handed to the magistrates, who sent them on to the owner. . . . You very soon see that you are among the most honest people in the world.[186]

—Charles Loring Brace

If this story is true, the Englishman believed these peasants were *more* honest than what he was accustomed to. If any reader were so inclined, he or she should not imagine that Nordic people are perfectly honest or that anyone else is completely dishonest. Here as elsewhere it is a matter of degree (not black and white, but shades of gray). And degrees matter—a molehill and a mountain are not equal.

In an example from the mid-1800s, a Swedish woman was interrogated about her religious beliefs by several high-ranking clergymen. She was a young rural woman, alone in a strange city, and the men questioning her were the highest-status men she would ever meet. When a bishop asked if it was true that she had called her pastor "ungodly," she answered *truthfully*: "Yes, and if I may say what I think, probably you all [including the bishop] are ungodly."[187]

If Scandinavian immigrants were honest and truthful it should be reflected in crime statistics, and apparently it is:

> [T]he reports of the penitentiary of Minnesota are more complete and thorough than those of similar institutions in neighboring states. . . . In 1882 the Canadian-born had one convict in "confinement" in the penitentiary to every 1,743 inhabitants . . . Germans and Irish had a proportion of one to 2,148 and one to 2,358 . . . Scandinavian-born had a proportion of one to 4,145.[188]

> —*O.N. Nelson*

That Nordic people continue to be honest and continue to speak truthfully is evident from question A165 of the world values surveys. When asked if most people can be trusted, the yes answers were: Denmark 67 percent, Sweden 66 percent, Norway 65 percent, Netherlands 60 percent, Finland 58 percent, New Zealand 48 percent, Iceland 41 percent, Canada 39 percent, United States 36 percent, Germany 35 percent, Italy 33 percent, Great Britain 30 percent, Russia 24 percent, and France 22 percent.[189] On average, more than twice as many Nordic people trust their neighbors as is true for the people of Italy, Great Britain, Russia, and France.

With equality, no one has authority over anyone else: all depend on each other. Honesty and truthfulness are necessary to keep society functioning. Today, some authorities believe that "trust" is one of the most important elements in the success of societies and of nations.[190]

Respect is an essential mutual responsibility, but it is generally acknowledged and not essential to this discussion, so it will be omitted here. Fairness and justice are important mutual responsibilities, and they are referred to in Chapter Ten.

> The ethics of the Havamal [Icelandic saga] are . . . rooted in belief in the value of the individual, who is nonetheless . . . tied by inextricable bonds to nature and society.[191]
>
> *—Matthias Sæmundsson*

Some readers might be asking themselves if there is an inherent conflict between the claims that, on the one hand, women (and men) were independent, and children at an early age became independent individuals, and on the other hand, that Nordic people accepted—without thinking—that they were part of a group and that they had mutual responsibilities. This possible conflict has not gone unnoticed. Author and Swedish scholar Marilyn McGriff mentioned, "A strong group identification combined with highly individualized accomplishments." Joy Ibsen, an author and also editor of *Church and Life* (a Danish-American publication), wrote of a "cooperative spirit and personal independence."[192] According to a survey, Norwegian parents would most like to pass on to their children the values of "independence and responsibility."[193] The words of H. Rider Haggard a century ago are worth repeating regarding "the [Danish] practice of general cooperation, to achieve individual and national success."[194]

Both independence and responsibility were clearly visible in sled dog musher Leonhard Seppala:

> I am proud of my racing trophies, but I would trade them all for the satisfaction of knowing that my dogs and I tried honestly to give our very best in humanitarian service to our fellowman . . .[195]

Seppala, a Finnish-Norwegian immigrant and arguably the greatest musher of all time, was given the most difficult and dangerous leg in the 1925 race to deliver diphtheria serum to Nome, Alaska. Seppala was an intense individual competitor (against the elements or against other racers), and he felt an intense responsibility to others.

"Independent individuals" and "mutual responsibilities" do not conflict—unless, one expresses one's individuality in a way that harms others.

With group identity, one knows (unconsciously, without thinking) that one is an equal member of a group. The group is helpful in many instances and absolutely necessary in others. Cooperation and consensus, honesty and truthfulness, and respect, together with fairness and justice, are not fluff. They are principles that make the group (society) work efficiently. They are fundamental to equality.

If no one has authority over anyone else, what happens when, inevitably, someone refuses to agree, or refuses to participate? Outside of legal constraints, if an individual wishes to thwart group action, or does not satisfy mutual responsibilities, the most effective tool available may be social pressure.[196] Social pressure as expressed in *Janteloven, lagom,* and *moderasjo* has been viewed by

Americans as a negative, although we also experience social pressure (based on different values).[197] Presumably, social pressure exists in all societies.

These responsibilities (cooperation, honesty, respect, justice, etc.) are principles that today are well-recognized because of their value to society. In the past, these principles made a good life possible in a harsh, stingy environment. Today, these Nordic principles are the basis of a progressive society.

A Long-Term Nordic Value: As equal members of a group, all share mutual responsibilities.

8

Practical Literature

Scandinavian stories [sagas] were more realistic with an infinitely longer perspective than feudal European stories. [198]

—*Mark Bloch*

In the past, Nordic literature was more practical than literature in other areas of Europe. *Practical* has synonyms such as *sober, rational, realistic*, and *pragmatic*. Any of these words would work, but *practical* was chosen because it is frequently used in the sources for this chapter. But here *practical* also implies *secular* because the contrast is often secular literature versus theological (or idealistic) literature.

Nordic literature may have been more practical because of equality and because of environment. For example, Nordic literature was created and handed down by ordinary people, most of whom were not completely settled, and who were themselves involved in the daily struggle for existence—their lives were on the line. At the same time, literature in feudal Europe was created and handed down by upper-class men, usually priests, who lived in areas with adequate cropland to support a sedentary population, and who were themselves divorced from the daily struggle for existence—their lives were not on the line.

The oldest surviving Nordic literature may be one of the Icelandic sagas known as *Ynglings saga.* This story describes two groups of pagan gods, the *Vanir* and the *Æsir,* who migrated (about 100 B.C.) to the Nordic area from Scythia north of the Black Sea. *Ynglings saga* is supernatural, but it contains valuable social and historical information, some of which (in secularized form) found its way into Anders Fryxell's 1840s' *History of Sweden.*[199]

Beowulf, set in Sweden and Denmark, was an oral story among the Angles, Saxons, and Jutes before they migrated in ships to England (Angle-land) around A.D. 450. It was written down in England in the eighth century and is considered to be the oldest extant "English" literature. It is impossible to date *Beowulf,* but it must come from before A.D. 450 and it appears to mention the same Danish royal family as is mentioned in *Ynglings saga. Beowulf* is supernatural literature, but the Nordic society depicted is realistic.

Oral literature of the Goths was recorded by Cassiodorus (a Roman senator) during the Folk-Wandering time (A.D. 400–650) when the Roman Empire was overrun by Huns from Asia and Goths from Scandinavia.[200] Cassiodorus published a Gothic history, but his books were lost. Fortunately, his work had already been copied by a Goth named Jordanes whose history contains a Gothic account of the great fifth-century battle between Goths and Huns on the Catalaunian Plains in France.[201]

The Gothic saga (literature) of this battle is not simple images of courageous warriors. This saga is written as straightforward history and includes strategy, intrigue, emotion, motivation, and psychology. It is not metaphysical and, apparently, it is not fabricated. It is a colorful but realistic (practical) account of an important event, 1560 years ago.

Völsunga (the saga of Sigurd/Siegfried) was preserved in several locations and is known by different names. It was especially popular in the Nordic region where there are, to this day, preserved wood carvings, stone carvings, and tapestries depicting scenes from this saga. *Völsunga* is metaphysical literature (Sigurd slays the dragon Fafnir) but it is also practical.

In this saga, set in continental Europe about A.D. 450, the hero Sigurd visits the warrior-maiden Brynhild and asks if she will teach him her wisdom. Brynhild responds by reciting a pre-Christian code of ethics which is 100 percent practical.[202] This pattern (literature containing metaphysical elements that are combined with a very practical message) is repeated off and on in Nordic literature for centuries. The essence appears to be: life contains metaphysical elements, but actions are always practical, and if there is conflict, practicality rules.[203]

Behave well towards your kinsmen and take but scant revenge on them for their offences. Bear with them, and you will win lasting praise. Be on your guard against things that are harmful, both against a maid's love and a man's wife, ill often comes of them. Don't argue much with fools at crowded meetings . . .[204]

—*Excerpt from Brynhild's advice to Sigurd*

A collection of poems, compiled and edited by Elias Lönnrot, was published before 1850 with the title *The Kalevala*. Most of these poems had roots among the Karelians who then lived in eastern Finland and neighboring areas of Russia. The poems are impossible to date, but no doubt many of them are ancient. *The Kalevala* bears some resemblance to *Beowulf* in that it is metaphysical literature, but it provides insight into society as it existed long ago.

In Iceland, from the 1100s into the 1300s, many old Nordic stories (sagas) were recorded. Often they related to the era when Iceland was founded, about A.D. 870. Iceland became Christian about A.D. 1000, and the Catholic Church used Latin, but that was not the language of the sagas. Rather, these sagas were recorded in Old Norse, the spoken language of ordinary people. Thus, they were recorded by people who worked—like everyone else—for their living, and they were meant to be read and enjoyed by ordinary people.[205]

Nordic people have long appreciated the Icelandic sagas, while, in the past, non-Nordic people often either were unaware of this great volume of literature or else they dismissed it as insignificant. That has changed in recent decades as a general appreciation of the sagas has replaced the earlier skepticism. Today the Icelandic sagas enjoy general respect in the non-Nordic world, and scholars of literature appreciate that, at the time they were written, they were unique. Nowhere else in Europe was anyone writing literature for ordinary people. The Icelandic sagas are straightforward, nuanced, complex, interesting, and socially and historically valuable. Compared to literature elsewhere in Europe, these sagas were secular and practical.[206]

Written about A.D. 1247 in Norway, *The King's Mirror* was composed as a dialogue between a wise father and his son who wishes to become a merchant. The anonymous author was "less bound" by theology:

> [The author's] outlook on the world is broader than that of most medieval writers. In matters of science he is less credulous and less bound by theological thought than others [elsewhere in Europe] who wrote on these subjects in his own century . . . on many subjects we find him giving utterance to thoughts which have a distinctly modern appearance. . . . But it is probably in the field of education where the great Northman is farthest in advance of his time. In his day the work of instruction was still in the hands of the church; and the churchmen showed no great anxiety to educate men except for the clerical profession.[207]

The author's "modern" advice includes: "wherever you are, be polite and agreeable," "make it a habit to rise early in the morning," "observe carefully how those who are reputed the best and most prominent merchants conduct their business," "be careful to examine the wares you buy before the purchase," and so forth.[208]

The King's Mirror author advises the young man to

be a good Christian, but the preponderance of the father's advice is secular. In ten pages of detailed advice on how to conduct oneself as a merchant, the author is first and foremost practical.[209]

At this point we will stop our investigation of Nordic literature. In a later chapter on government (authority, laws, and institutions), evidence will be presented that Nordic people continued to be practical. They were Christians, but, as had always been the case, they were also preoccupied with the necessities of life. When a conflict arose between religious teachings and practical actions—practical came first.[210]

As mentioned earlier, most literature in feudal Europe was created by upper-class men, often priests, who were insulated from the daily struggle for the necessities of life. Their writings were intended to be read by other upper-class men. Some stories were written in the vernacular and some in Latin, which was not in use outside of the Catholic Church.

For centuries before and after Nordic sagas were recorded in Iceland, ordinary people in central and southern Europe as well as Russia were illiterate. Many of their lords were illiterate. Priests were sometimes literate in the local language and usually literate in Latin. A few secular poems and songs were handed down, word of mouth, and for centuries that was the extent of secular literature.[211]

The priests' principal concern was theology, and many of the most talented among them were preoccupied with the end-time, the study of which is known as *eschatology*.[212] Learned priests studied and meditated on this subject for years or decades, and they wrote about it.

Priests also sometimes wrote "history," but their history was almost pure fiction. They were the most respected members of their community, and yet they felt no need to adhere to truth or facts. A date and place for an event might be correct, but everything else was fabricated. Numbers in these "histories" are meaningless; "100,000 people" might actually have been one thousand or none at all. In the same way, priests as well as ordinary people were indifferent to the passage of time. They knew they were near the end of time—that was all that mattered.[213]

The Italian poet Dante (1265–1321) wrote the *Divine Comedy*, an immensely popular work, which is roughly contemporary with the recording of the Icelandic sagas.

[T]he theme is Dante's journey through hell, purgatory, and paradise. . . . Hell and purgatory are treated as geographical facts. Hell is directly beneath Jerusalem, the center of the land-hemisphere. It is a hollow inverted cone . . . divided into nine concentric ledges, each devoted to the punishment of a distinct class of sinners. At the apex of the cone, the center of gravity, Lucifer is fixed in eternal ice. Purgatory is a lofty conical mountain rising from an island in the southern hemisphere. . . . [consisting] of seven concentric terraces, on each of which one of the seven deadly sins is expiated. At the summit of the mountain is the earthly paradise, the original Eden . . . nine heavens.[214]

A Spanish contemporary of Shakespeare, Cervantes published his classic *Don Quixote* in 1605. This story is humor: it is a satire of the "romances of chivalry." It provides a picture of society at that time, but the hero is a knight. *Don Quixote* is secular but it is not realistic; it does not represent real life for ordinary people.

Shakespeare was an English playwright in the decades before and after 1600. His father was illiterate, and Shakespeare's plays could be enjoyed by ordinary people. His plays contained metaphysical elements but they were secular. Generally, his works do not represent real life for ordinary people. They were—arguably—entertainment.

John Milton was a well-educated English Puritan who wrote in both Latin and English. His classic, *Paradise Lost*, published in 1667, describes a titanic struggle between God and Satan; it is metaphysical and not biblical.

> [In *Paradise Lost*, Milton took] his own positions on the Trinity, the divinity of Christ and the Holy Ghost, predestination, the creation of the world, etc.[215]

Theology-based literature (Dante and Milton) was the rule in their time, but a century after *Paradise Lost* was published the philosophy of the Enlightenment (see Chapter Ten) was urging that theology should be disentangled from civic and political life in feudal Europe:

> [T]he beginning of the modern period of secular culture, in contrast to the theological spirit that constituted the regularizing principal of society in the previous epoch.[216]

"Regularizing principal" is the key here: theology had *regulated* every aspect of people's lives. The Enlightenment

83

did not attempt to eliminate theology; it attempted to eliminate or reduce theology's control over society and government. The Enlightenment brought feudal Europe closer to Nordic culture.[217]

This brief inquiry for the feudal era (A.D. 800–1789) reveals significant differences between Nordic literature and literature from the rest of Europe. For most of this period, in central and southern Europe and in Russia, ordinary people were illiterate. Writers were upper class, and they wrote for other members of their class; most literature was theological and other writings, represented as history, were idealized fabrications with only a kernel of truth. The writers of the Enlightenment idealized rural ordinary people. Near the end of this period, secular literature appeared and it sometimes contained messages, but it was generally entertainment. In some cases it was enjoyed by ordinary people, but it was not reality for them.

During this period in the Nordic region, Christianity was well established and Latin was its language, but the Nordic sagas and other Nordic literature were written in Old Norse with ordinary people as the intended audience.[218] Nordic literature often contained a message and it was usually practical.

Foreign visitors sometimes observed differences in literature. An English war correspondent in Russia in 1905 reported:

> [T]he book I found that they nearly all of them read was Milton's *Paradise Lost*. . . . They [Russian peasants] like the narrative of supernatural events which combine the fantasy of a fairy tale and

the authority of Scriptures—the school-master in Tambov told me that the peasants refused to read historical novels or stories because they said they were "Vydumke" (inventions) . . .[219]

—Maurice Baring

A Nordic visitor to England and its American colonies in 1748 observed:

With respect to the nation's [England's] taste for literature, little books of comedies, tragedies, novels, etc., seem to be preferred, that is books that entertain and amuse.[220]

—Peter Kalm

Like Kalm in the 1700s, an English visitor in the early 1900s also noticed a difference:

And by the way, every little town in Denmark has several newspapers, rather better than ours in places of similar size, since they carry more world news and no so-called 'comics.'[221]

—Harry A. Franck

A Long-Term Nordic Value: A good story is realistic and contains a message.

9
Practical Thinking

If "culture" is an elusive and slippery subject, attempting to examine how a whole people "think" is worse. Because there is little direct evidence, now or in the past, related to "thinking," this chapter will examine how organized and resourceful people were. "Organized" includes (but is not limited to) being conscious of time, which some social scientists correlate with progress.[222] "Resourceful" is how people respond to their environment: how carefully, or successfully, do they exploit available (including distant) resources?

To whatever extent a people systematically (and creatively) exploit resources; to whatever extent they are fully aware of the passage of time; to whatever extent they anticipate, by their actions, future needs and contingencies—to that extent we will imagine that they are employing *practical thinking*.[223]

Organized and resourceful (as evidence of practical thinking) should not be confused with what is sometimes referred to as a "work ethic" or as the "Protestant work ethic." This concept was the creation of German sociologist Max Weber (1864–1920). Weber theorized that the Calvinist belief in predestination correlated with the rise of capitalism; according to him, the fatalistic attitude implied by predestination was a good fit for capitalism.[224]

Later writers, recognizing that Weber's theory was too narrow (many people were not Calvinists), expanded his concept into a "Protestant work ethic." This appeared to have merit because capitalism worked well in the Protestant countries and people there were generally industrious workers. Later, when Americans observed that Scandinavian immigrants, most of them Protestant, were trustworthy and industrious workers, it was attributed to their "work ethic."

Weber's theory was too narrow, and a Protestant work ethic is not the subject of this chapter. Imagine for a moment: what if Catholicism embodied southern European values (including stratified society) and the Protestant Reformation discarded southern European values in favor of northern European values (emphasis on the individual and bottom-up authority)? Luther taught that everyone was a priest, and everyone should have access to the Bible—that is certainly bottom-up.[225] And Luther stressed the importance of educating children, which was long considered a necessity in the Nordic area.[226]

Maybe what appeared to be a work ethic was not a product of either Calvinism or Protestantism. But, whether that is true or not is irrelevant here, because, in the Nordic area, theology did not usually control secular activities (they were separate), and "work ethic" is something different from "practical thinking."[227]

[1856] We compared their [Swedish workers'] cheerful, healthy faces, with the worn faces of English "factories," and the aspect of certain position and dignity in them with the usual expression of depressed toil in working women.[228]

—Charles Loring Brace

Question A030 on the *Human Beliefs and Values* surveys asks whether it is particularly important that children be taught the value of hard work. Those who answered yes: Denmark 2 percent, Sweden 4 percent, Norway 11 percent, Finland 12 percent, Netherland 14 percent, Germany 23 percent, Iceland 44 percent, Canada 53 percent, United States 61 percent, and Russia 91 percent.[229] However, these responses are misleading because in the Nordic countries it is assumed that people will take care of themselves, one is not supposed to ask for help, and children know they will be independent at an early age. Hard work, by itself, is not a Nordic value, but it might be necessary to satisfy other values.

[In Norway] No one's going to sneer at you if you don't want to work weekends, don't covet that promotion, if you choose to have a life.[230]

—Paul Kirby

Immigrant letters sometimes mentioned that it was necessary to work harder in the New World than it had been at home. It would be practical to work as hard as was necessary to reach one's goals. It would be honest to do the work that one had agreed to. Everyone needed to be independent and care for his or her own needs. Probably, the apparent "work ethic" of Nordic immigrants included several values, and the immigrants seldom valued hard work for its own sake.[231]

[1930, Finland] Tampere's factories would hardly be recognized as non-American, except for the sense of unlimited leisure hanging over them . . . [They] have every modern convenience and up-to-date method; but even in the workrooms time is not at a premium.[232]

—*Harry A. Franck*

In central Europe and Russia during the early and middle feudal era, people *knew* that they were living at the end of time.[233] Their time horizon, ahead and behind, was short. History went back a few centuries at most, and the world would end any day now. To the extent one thought about time at all, it was in cycles: the growth cycle of plants, the lunar (monthly) cycle, the solar (yearly) cycle, the cycle of a human life, and so on. The concept of linear time, progress, would have been completely foreign.

The good fortune or bad fortune that one experienced was the result of a constant battle between the forces of good and evil. Demons, saints, and angels perpetually struggled, and the ebb and flow of that struggle was evident in storms, famines, pestilence, and wars.[234] God would provide, and the end was near. Meek acceptance was more reasonable than attempting to plan ahead and influence events by one's own actions.[235]

[1860s] [T]he settled population of Siberia, including the Russians . . . might catch and dry fish enough in one year to last them three; but instead of doing this, they barely provide food enough to last them through one winter, and take the chances of starvation on the next. No experience, however severe, no suffering, however great, ever teaches them prudence.[236]

—*George Keenan*

During the feudal era, ordinary people were ruled by different levels of authority. They were told what to do, and they had little or no influence on the decisions that ruled their lives. There was little reason to even think. But, conditions gradually changed. The Protestant Reformation (early sixteenth century) produced changes. Feudalism gradually lost its grip in France before the revolution (late eighteenth century). Social movements in England and elsewhere also produced changes. However, change was slower in Germany where a mid-nineteenth century social revolution failed, and slower still in Russia where alcohol may have played a role.[237]

Russia extends as far north as the Nordic countries (Moscow is the same latitude as the southern border of Denmark), but most of its farmland has an adequate growing season, and there was no shortage of Russian cropland; Russians were not dependent on livestock.[238] Central and southern Europe are farther south than Russia, and here also cropland was adequate and people were less dependent on livestock.

Generally, in central and southern Europe as well as Russia, adequate cropland with a normal growing season allowed people to not only produce enough food for themselves but also to produce enough to support a nonproductive upper class. Ordinary people had almost no input into the decisions that affected their daily lives. There was no reason people had to think practically.

> [1748, Englishmen] could spend often the greater part of the day [in a pub] . . . It is not to be wondered at then, if a great many labourers and others, however large the daily wages and profits they can make, can, for all that, scarcely collect more than what goes from hand to mouth.[239]

> *—Peter Kalm*

Chapter Three (Independent Women) contains a brief argument that evidence of nomadic herder culture (Scythians and others) might be relevant to ancient Nordic culture. Repeated waves of these nomads migrated into Europe from the Eurasian steppe— and when people migrate they bring their culture with them (Scandinavian immigrants' culture is still visible in many of their American descendants).

Nomadic herders moved their cattle, sheep, and horses to distant grazing areas for the warm months of the year, and then returned with their animals to areas sheltered from storms for the winter. They carried with them everything they owned. Their livestock grazed as they traveled and, frequently, different groups used the same trails and forded rivers at the same locations. Nomadic herders needed to schedule their movements and coordinate with other groups, and they needed to ensure that no one group used up all of the pasture. To avoid conflict, they needed to be (and were) highly organized.[240]

The Nordic physical environment is unique. Here, firm, dry land is everywhere divided and subdivided by waterways. Travel by water was absolutely necessary; Nordic people needed to build boats and they needed to navigate (find their way from place to place). Needing to travel by water was both an opportunity and a challenge. It was a challenge because one had to plan ahead for long distance travel. Imagine the thought and planning that went into a Viking expedition. Without knowing exactly what conditions would be encountered, it was necessary to carry along on the ship most of the things that might be needed for weeks of sailing. And Vikings needed to be skilled and experienced at navigating. Where more than one ship was involved, organization and planning was magnified by the number of ships. Nordic life during the Viking era and continuing up to the modern era was complex—it required practical thinking.[241]

And waterways were an opportunity: they were the roads and highways that connected Nordic people to the rest of Europe, or to western Asia, or to North America. The need to use boats and ships, the need to navigate, and the exposure to different peoples and different cultures influenced Nordic thinking. Today, colleges sometimes require that students study abroad for a certain length of time. It is generally believed that visiting and living with different people in a different culture is an enriching experience—educational. No doubt that was as true in the past as it is today, and Nordic people did much more traveling than other Europeans.

[Danish] mariners sailed on long voyages . . . people were wont to travel to an extent hard to credit nowadays, and on foot. These journeys were often over astonishing distances . . .[242]

—*Peter Michelsen and Holger Rasmussen*

Everyday life demanded planning and organization. Fields were small and the growing season was short. Crops had to be planted on time and harvested on time. Because of the shortage of good cropland, Nordic people were more dependent on livestock than other Europeans. But cows produced most of their milk during a few months in the summer. They had to have good pasture during that period, and their milk had to be preserved by making it into cheeses and butter. Winter feed for animals had to be harvested and preserved for the long winter ahead. There was no time to waste. Famine was normal and recurring; failure to accomplish tasks on time increased the chances that one would starve.

[1904] The power of organization in a highly developed degree is another characteristic feature of the Swedish nation . . .[243]

—*Gustav Sundbärg*

Except in areas with significant amounts of fertile cropland, Nordic people, in spite of differences in wealth and status, were social equals. There were classes, but they were narrow. Most people lived the same, dressed the same, and made their living doing the same activities. Decision making where people are equals could be compared to what businessmen today call "flat" management. For Nordic people, management was completely flat—the people making the decisions were the same people who were affected by the decisions. There was no chain of command. Decision making (thinking) had an immediate effect on those who were doing it.

Somehow, a written chart of an annual work schedule for a Nordic husband and wife was preserved, circa A.D. 1750:[244]

	Wife	Husband
January	Household work; care for livestock; spin & weave; prepare hemp; break branches (fodder)	Cut wood; haul hay, wood & branches; trip to market [more than 100 miles]
February	Household work, care for livestock, spin, thrash	Forge iron tools; cut & haul wood & branches; trip to market
March	Household work; live-stock; spin	Cut wood; haul wood and branches; market
April	Household work; care for livestock; spin, weave	Haul branches, wood and hay; burn stubble fields; haul manure
May	Household work; care for livestock; baking for summer	Haul wood & branches; clean & clear ditches; fieldwork, sowing
June	Harvest birch bark; household work; care for livestock	Put up bog iron; repair boats, hay barns, tools; make charcoal, lime & tar; fish; get birch bark; move cattle to pasture
July	Make hay; household work; care for livestock	Hay mountain swamps, meadows, and pastures

The chart continues on for the remaining five months and includes activities such as slaughter, sheep shearing, flax processing, and more. "Household work" was making cheese, churning butter, cooking, sewing, knitting, caring for children and the sick, washing clothes and dishes, cleaning, and more. "Care for livestock" included milking, herding, cleaning barn, and feeding.

The husband and wife on this chart were ordinary people; Americans would refer to them as "farmers." They were highly organized, and they carefully exploited all of the resources available to them: fields exploited for grain, hay, and pasture; meadows and swamps exploited for pasture, hay, and bog iron; forests exploited for pasture, firewood, lumber, wood for tools, branches for fodder, charcoal, and birch bark; streams and lakes exploited for fish. They manufactured (from scratch) tools, implements, utensils, clothing—you name it—and they traded with others.

> [W]hen there is a conflict between practicality and other values, the other values give way.[245]
>
> —*David Jenkins*

Practical thinking is visible in the actions of young Nordic women who emigrated. They decided to leave family, friends, and homeland to improve their lives, but emigration was just the first step.[246] Often, when they first arrived they would try to live with a relative or friend for a few months to learn the culture (what was expected). Then they would find work as a domestic with a family that had young children who could help them learn English. Frequently they had a working knowledge of English within a few months and then they were free to shop for the best possible position. Circumstances varied with each immigrant, but as a rule, the decisions they made were practical.[247]

Generally, Nordic immigrants' expectations about what they would find in the New World were realistic.[248] There were exceptions, those who believed that the streets were paved with gold, but they were a small minority. Most Nordic immigrants had read or heard accounts sent home from earlier immigrants, they had listened to returned emigrants, they were aware of prevailing wage rates, and they had an understanding of the job market or the availability of land.[249] And, practicality had always required Nordic people to exploit distant resources, which included leaving their home district to find work.

Emigration to America was an employment-seeking trip that was longer than usual.[250]

—*Reino Kero*

From 1825 to 1930 Europeans and Americans were interested in polar exploration— an interest that was focused on reaching both of the earth's poles and also on finding the long-sought Northwest Passage (a shipping shortcut across northern Canada). Many polar expeditions were either English or Nordic. England had a much larger population than the combined Nordic countries, and the British Empire was near its zenith, but English polar expeditions were sometimes tragic and always less successful than Nordic expeditions.

Nordic explorers Amundsen, Freuchen, Nansen, Stefansson, and Nordenskjöld, together with Orkney native

John Rae, had no equals in England or anywhere else. The expeditions led by these men were successful because they employed practical thinking (being organized) while English explorers did not.[251] The English upper class knew that their culture was innately superior.[252] They did not need to carefully study information from earlier expeditions; they did not need to consider the unique conditions they would encounter in the polar regions. They did not need to *think*.

"Practical thinking" is true, but it's not the whole story. The upper-class English explorers could not use indigenous (Sami, Inuit, Indian) technology—that would have meant that they "were going native." Nordic people believed in equality, and Nordic expeditions succeeded because they used indigenous technology (skis, dogs, dogsleds, kayaks, clothing, food, etc.).[253]

Stories contain clues as to how people think. One such is a Nordic folk tale of three brothers, the youngest of whom is the hero. He is not the first to take action or the first to deal with issues, but he is always "creative and observant." In Nordic stories such as this the people who cause difficulties are officials (including clergymen).[254]

In a story from *Nordic Views and Values*, a servant with a strong desire to improve his position in life investigates the practicality of becoming a farm owner by creating a new farm out of a swamp. He thoroughly examines the soil in the swamp, and he carefully examines how the swamp could be drained. Then he and his wife, at great length, discuss all of the issues relating to this project.[255]

The preceding chapter provided evidence that Nordic literature was practical. If that was true, it naturally follows that their literature reflected people's thinking. Nordic people and their stories were realistic, and they were firmly rooted in time.[256] They were aware of the distant past, and they carefully planned for the future.

> [1904, Folk Schools] only exist in the three kingdoms of Scandinavia and also in Finland. Their purpose is to furnish adult members, especially the peasantry, with an education at once civil, patriotic, and practical. [257]
>
> —*Gustav Sundbärg*

> [T]he Swede's foremost characteristic is a pronounced devotion to unemotional practicality . . .[258]
>
> —*David Jenkins*

> [T]he Danish view of life is hard headed, practical, and down to earth.[259]
>
> —*Steven M. Borish*

> The success of Finland . . . has been built upon flexibility and solution-orientation in all aspects of society.[260]
>
> —*Pasi Sahlberg*

A Long-term Nordic Value: All things considered, what works best?

10

Authority, Laws, and Institutions

When one, without thinking, knows that ordinary people have authority and that law and justice trump personal loyalty, then these are values—they are part of culture.

At his best man is the noblest of animals; separated from law and justice he is the worst.

—*Aristotle*

Twenty-five hundred years ago, based on archeological evidence, people in the Nordic area and in northwestern Germany were equal, while southern Europe had highly visible social classes.[261] Assuming that French sociologist Emmanuel Todd was correct (politics mirrors society), it is safe to say that political authority in the Nordic region belonged to the people, and in southern Europe political authority came from the top.[262]

Roman historian Tacitus described authority, laws, and institutions for ancient Nordic people:

[A.D. 98] They choose their kings by birth, their generals for merit. These kings have not unlimited or arbitrary power, and the generals do more by example than by authority. . . . About minor matters the chiefs deliberate, about the more important the whole tribe. Yet even when the final decision rests with the people, the affair is always thoroughly discussed by the chiefs. They assemble, except in case of emergency, on certain fixed days, either at new or at full moon. . . . When the multitude thinks proper, they sit down armed. Silence is proclaimed by the priests who have on these occasions the right of keeping order. Then the king, or the chief, according to age, birth, distinction in war, or eloquence, is heard, more because he has influence to persuade than because he has power to command. If his sentiments displease them, they reject them with murmurs; if they are satisfied they brandish their spears.[263]

The "institutions" mentioned by Tacitus are assemblies, kings, generals, chiefs, and priests. Based on their duties, Tacitus' "priests" apparently evolved into the lawspeaker of Viking times. In a later passage Tacitus described another institution: "In these same councils they also elect the chief magistrate, who administers the law . . . [and he] has a hundred associates chosen from the people who support him with their advice and influence."[264]

Regardless of any connection they might have claimed with some deity, kings were chosen by birth; they came from certain families. These kings did not have "unlimited or arbitrary power"—their authority was restricted.

Tacitus mentioned "the law," and in other passages he mentioned law in connection with marriage and inheritance. Probably the priest in Tacitus' time, and certainly the lawspeaker in Viking times, who kept order at the assembly, had memorized the laws.[265] Laws were not written, but they were specific and they were handed down from one generation to the next.

Tacitus did not explicitly mention women taking part in the assemblies. However, he mentions that the "whole tribe" deliberated and one of the subheadings of his account is, "Government. Influence of women." Tacitus also described women as partners of their husband and as being responsible for "management of the household, of the home, and of the land."[266] In one way or another, ancient Nordic women had political influence.

The assemblies, later known as "*ting*," were monthly ("at a new or full moon") or they could be convened in case of an emergency. From later evidence, a *ting* was both a legislative and judicial institution. Tacitus wrote, "Thus the sentiments of all having been discovered and laid bare . . . the final decision rests with the people." He was describing democratic government where authority belonged to the people, and if authority belonged to the people as a group, then laws and institutions were a practical way to solve conflicts, a practical way to maintain peace, order, and a civil society.

The authority, laws, and institutions described by Tacitus were still recognizable seven hundred years later at the beginning of the official Viking Era.[267] But there are many more sources available concerning the Vikings: the writings of outsiders as well as the sagas. *King Olafs saga* has a classic description of a Nordic assembly, *ting*, which was reportedly set in the year A.D. 1018. This account highlights an issue neglected by Tacitus: what was done about a king who abused his authority?

> But if you [the Swedish king] will not do as we desire, we will now attack you and kill you, for we will no longer allow you to break the law and disturb the peace. So our forefathers did when they drowned five kings . . . Then the king stood up and spoke and said that it would be done as the farmers wished. . . . [they could] rule on all matters that they were inclined to.[268]

> *—Snorri*

People at a *ting* claimed that the king "broke the law," and consequently, they had a right to do something about it.

Five hundred years after the Vikings, *tings* were still used, and based on that period, knowledgeable present-day writers have mentioned the concept that Nordic people as a group had authority and that they "contracted" with a king.[269] They gave part of their authority to the king, and in return he had responsibilities to them. There were powerful Viking kings, but ordinary people believed that they—the people—were the ultimate authority.

> [Vikings had] a most elaborate system of law and legal procedure.[270]

> *—Charles Homer Haskins*

In the time of Tacitus, or in the Viking era, or five hundred years ago, if ordinary people as a group had authority, effective laws and institutions were necessary. And beyond that, Nordic people, then and now, place a high value on justice; their long-established laws and institutions were and are designed to produce justice.

[Swedish proverbs contain] an extraordinary demand for justice. . . . Each person should be treated fairly.[271]

—*Fredrik Ström*

Propped on its four great pillars is Heaven's throne

But earthly crowns are stablished on Law alone

Where force does sway the Council, there lurks disaster,

But Justice decks with honour both Land and Master.[272]

—*Frithiofs Saga*

The sagas also describe a jury. *Eyrbyggja Saga* (fictionalized history written in the mid-1200s) mentioned a twelve-man jury in Iceland in the 870s. Apparently, the author of this saga believed that juries existed at that time.[273] *Ynglings saga*, which might date to 100 B.C., mentioned that twelve priests judged.[274] (Present-day jurors "judge" the evidence.)

The Northmen [Vikings] brought with them into Ireland the ideas of cities, commerce, and municipal life, hitherto unknown. . . . [They introduced laws] for municipal, rural, or social regulations; and . . . the spirit of commerce and enterprise.[275]

—*Aug. J. Thebaud*

In "the large egalitarian area" (roughly, the northern half of Sweden, western Finland, and most of Norway),[276] most of the people were owners of a small parcel of land, or they were the children of those owners. Among these people, the values that have been discussed endured uninterrupted.[277]

[A] basic trait of Finnish personality, the reluctance to submit to being ordered about by others.

—*Hans Wasastjerna*

In the centuries after the introduction of Christianity, in Nordic areas with expansive areas of good farmland, aristocratic landlords took root and prospered. These aristocrats, buttressed by law, usurped some authority that had long been held by ordinary people. Aristocratic landlords were found in southern Sweden, southern Finland, coastal areas of Norway, and all over Denmark. In these areas— because of powerful landlords—ordinary Nordic people, superficially at least, began to resemble other Europeans.[278]

In the Nordic region, aristocratic landlords were never as large, and never as removed from ordinary people as was true in other areas of Europe. In spite of the strong influence of these aristocrats in the regions mentioned above, and in spite of feudal or near-feudal conditions, Nordic culture persisted in these regions.[279] And, there was, as there always had been, interaction between the equal areas and the areas dominated by powerful landlords. Aristocrats constantly tried to increase their power, while the ordinary people under them pushed back, aware that other Nordic people were not subject to powerful landlords and believing that authority rightfully belonged to them.[280]

We are all priests.[281]

—Martin Luther

An early 1500s' religious movement led to a break with Catholicism. Those who broke away were Protestants, and their religious beliefs had political implications. Protestants emphasized individualism; everyone was to read the Bible him- or herself; people were responsible for their own churches.[282] This was a clear break with Catholicism's top-down authority. The Reformation succeeded in areas that had been influenced by ancient Nordic people.

Protestantism has taken hold chiefly of the Germanic [ancient Nordic] or Teutonic races, and is strongest in Germany, Switzerland, Scandinavia, Holland, the British Empire, and North America.[283]

A century ago, authorities often wrote of "races," but both Nordic people and other Europeans were mixtures of different groups. They were not races.

Protestant beliefs implied a change in culture (from top-down to bottom-up authority). That change was clearly stated by philosopher Johannes Althusius in his book *Politica*, published in 1603. He wrote that ordinary people are the source of power—as a group they have authority. Their authority can be given to a king in a contract, but if he rules poorly, if he ignores the contract, it can be broken. Althusius attributes his philosophy to earlier writers including ancient Greeks. Two later Nordic writers, Laurentius Paulinus Gothus (published 1617–1639) and Johannes Canuti Lenæeus (published 1633–1634), echoed Althusius, describing what, in essence, was an ancient Nordic attitude.[284]

Generally, in central and southern Europe from the thirteenth through the eighteenth centuries, feudalism was loosening its grip; it became necessary to establish effective laws and institutions that could replace the personal authority of princes, nobility, landlords, and patriarchs. In Russia during this period, feudalism did not loosen its grip, but, influenced by the rest of Europe, czars attempted (without much success) to establish effective laws and institutions.

> [A.D. 1247] Finally, remember this, that whenever you have an hour to spare you should give thought to your studies, especially to the [Nordic] law books.[285]

> —*The King's Mirror*

In the Nordic region, effective laws and institutions did not need to be established—they had a long history.[286] The names and duties of institutions sometimes changed or evolved; laws could be and were changed, but Nordic attitude toward authority, laws, and institutions did not change. There was a similar political system in the whole Nordic region, and that system included both effective laws and effective institutions. Nordic laws, which had earlier been memorized by lawspeakers, were written down in the

1200s.[287] They were written in the vernacular, the language of ordinary people. Law and justice were of primary importance to ordinary Nordic people.[288]

[W]e can find farmers quoting or referring quite fluently to paragraphs from the thirteenth century [Norwegian] national law . . .[289]

—*Magne Njåstad*

The ancient *ting* were still doing business.[290] A detailed account of one *ting* from the mid-1500s reveals several interesting details. Every free person was eligible to participate including women. Women played a smaller role than men, but they were not excluded. A non-landowner with sound reasoning and public speaking skills might play a more influential role than many landowners. This particular *ting* debated and voted to oppose their powerful king. The decision had to be unanimous. After they reached a consensus, they signed their names in a circle with no beginning or end. They were taking action as a group of equals.[291]

All voices count.[292]

—*Sverige & Svenskarna*

People as a group had authority, but they delegated part of their authority to a king who was obligated to the people in a number of ways, including listening to their grievances.[293] A recent scholarly study from a less egalitarian Nordic area in the 1500s found that tenant farmers regularly appealed directly to their king for redress on taxes, rents, or other issues. The farmers' petitions, especially when conditions were difficult, often were decided in favor of the tenants. In this less-egalitarian area, tenant farmers were not passive objects, and an "interdependency of king and crown peasantry was taken for granted."[294]

Property rights relate to laws and institutions. Into the 1800s, some Nordic non-tillable areas were communal as they always had been. With that exception, Nordic people were individuals, and they had individual rights to property.[295] Viking ships were owned by one or more individuals. Nordic homes, farm fields, and livestock were individually owned. When industry developed in the Nordic regions (ironworks, grain mills, sawmills, etc.) it was privately owned. In the 1800s Nordic cooperatives were established, but they too were privately owned; individuals held shares in them.

Possibly as a long-term side effect of extended families, in central Europe during the feudal era, property was often communally owned. Tillable fields, pastures, and hay fields, and businesses such as bakeries, flour mills, blacksmith shops, and other property were communally owned.[296] Businesses were not only communally owned—they were communally maintained. In Russia, peasants believed that God should own land, not people.[297] As feudalism gradually lost control in central Europe, and because of social revolutions, communal property gave way to private property. But, for the people of central Europe and Russia, a change in attitude toward property was necessary before they became "modern." In the Nordic region, no change was necessary.

During this period, national assemblies and other institutions emerged. There was an ongoing competition for political power among ordinary people, the clergy, the aristocracy, and the kings. This competition for power involved changing alliances among the players, and it occasionally was influenced by the old Nordic warrior-farmer tradition.

Assemblies, similar to the Nordic *ting*, were common in England until the Norman invasion (A.D. 1066) greatly curtailed Nordic traditions there.[298] But northern Germany as well as North Sea coastal lands including the Netherlands, where the ancient warrior-farmer tradition survived, successfully resisted feudalism for centuries, and besides never experienced it to the same degree as most of Europe.[299]

In the Nordic egalitarian area, the warrior-farmer tradition had never ceased. Raiding stopped by about A.D. 1100, probably as a response to Christianity, but ordinary people were still armed. And they influenced political developments in the whole Nordic region.

> [T]he aristocracy . . . endeavored to put into force . . . the principles of feudalism. The Swedish peasantry averted this danger by rising in arms [1434] . . . the peasants in conjunction with the patriotic section of the nobility . . . [were] the ruling caste.[300]
>
> —*Gustav Sundbärg*

In 1743, 4,500 armed farmers marched into Stockholm. The marchers were peaceful, but the sight of that many armed men made the other players more sympathetic to ordinary people.[301]

The source of authority was a central theme of the Enlightenment as expressed by such philosophers as John Locke (1632–1704), Francois Voltaire (1694–1778), and Jean Jacques Rousseau (1712–1778). They directly challenged the long-held feudal assumption that authority came from above:

> [Rousseau's] Contat Social, as the name implies, endeavors to base all government on the consent, direct or implied, of the governed.[302]

Rousseau claimed that authority came from ordinary people, that government was based "on the consent, direct or implied, of the governed." That sounds very much like American democracy and the U.S. Constitution, which begins with "We the people . . . do ordain and establish . . ." People had authority, and that was directly opposite of contemporary English government where King George III had authority.

But the Enlightenment had little if any effect in the Nordic region.[303] Thirty years before Locke was born and more than a century before Rousseau, philosopher Johannes Althusius had argued that authority belonged to ordinary people as a group; essentially, he restated an ancient Nordic value.[304] Among ancient Nordic people nineteen centuries ago, "the final decision rests with the people."

In the 1700s, concurrent with the Enlightenment and the American Revolution, social revolutions erupted in Europe. Illustrating a typical contrast in these revolutions, the Danes outlawed feudalism without bloodshed, but a couple of years later in 1789, bloodshed was a hallmark of the French Revolution. Except for a civil war in Finland in 1918 (possibly influenced by the Russian Revolution), Nordic social revolutions were gradual and mostly bloodless, while other European social revolutions, including Russia in 1918, involved armed insurrection.

Why were the Nordic social revolutions generally peaceful? Undoubtedly, one reason is that most Nordic aristocrats were not as far removed from ordinary people as was true elsewhere in Europe.[305] For example, the first language of the Russian aristocracy was French, and some Russian aristocrats did not even speak Russian.

Another possible reason was shared Nordic culture:[306]

Strained relations between the different social classes in Sweden [and other Nordic countries] have, however, been mitigated, by that fellow-feeling which . . . is a characteristic trait running through all classes of the community.[307]

—Gustav Sundbärg

"Fellow-feeling" in this quote is a well-recognized Nordic value that elsewhere in these pages is referred to as "group identity." The key in this quote is "running through *all classes*." This is a plausible explanation of why Nordic social revolutions were mostly peaceful.

As late as the 1700s in much of central and southern Europe and into the twentieth century in Russia, authority was top-down. Most "laws" were local custom, as well as people could remember it.[308] But courts were controlled by aristocrats, so laws were meaningless window dressing. Other institutions such as public meetings and various officials were controlled by the aristocracy, and these institutions facilitated top-down authority. Here, ordinary people had no real political power (authority); when conditions became unbearable they resorted to violence. Their options were: quietly endure or revolt.

In the Nordic region, by ancient tradition, authority resided in the people, with laws and institutions to ensure justice and peace. In areas where an aristocracy developed, ordinary people's political, economic, and social status was eroded, but people's culture (attitudes and values) did not change. In the large egalitarian area, people retained their authority, they were self-governing at the local level, and they believed that the king held his authority through them. He was responsible to them. In the end, this area influenced the less-egalitarian areas.

> [T]he question to be raised . . . is not primarily whether the common man could influence state policy and legislation, but rather how he did so . . .[309]

— *Peter Blickle, Steven Ellis, Eva Österberg*

In most of Europe, it was necessary to develop new laws, new institutions, and a new attitude toward authority. In the Nordic region, effective laws and institutions already existed alongside a modern attitude toward authority. Today, the ancient *ting* is visible in names such as *Folketing* (Denmark's parliament), *Storting* (Norway's parliament), *Althing* (Iceland's parliament), and *Tingsrätt* (Finland's court system).[310]

Readers who would like to learn more about authority, laws, and institutions in the Nordic countries (and their neighbors) are urged to read the contributions of Katajal, Gustafsson, Johansson, Njåstad, Juliusson, et al. in *Northern Revolts*, edited by Kimmo Katajal. Similarly, the essays by Imsen and Günter as well as Blickle, Ellis, and Österberg in *Resistance, Representation, and Community*, edited by Peter Blickle, are well worth reading.

Authority determined who got fresh horses. Centuries ago, a "post" system existed in Europe where a traveler could obtain fresh horses to continue a long journey. A tale involving this post system illustrates how Nordic attitude differed from their neighbors. One day in the 1800s, a Nordic farmer driving a rough wagon stopped at a post station for fresh horses. There were only two left, and while they were being harnessed, a high government official drove up and demanded to have those fresh horses. The farmer refused, saying that he had arrived first. The official conceded— there was nothing he could do.[311]

If this tale had been set in Russia on the same day, the outcome would have been different. The man would have not only given up the fresh horses, but he would have also shown deference. Perhaps he would have removed his cap, bowed at the waist, and uttered, "Yes my lord," while he handed over the horses. Not only did the official have the right to take any post horses, he also had the right to take horses from any peasants he encountered. Russian officials had authority; Russian peasants did not.[312]

Justice in the life and conduct of the state is possible only as first it resides in the hearts and souls of the citizens.

—Plato

Scandinavian immigrants had long believed that authority resided in the people (democracy), they believed in laws and justice, and they were accustomed to self-government. A Norwegian-American author wrote of the immigrants:

[They] take as naturally to politics as goslings do to water.[313]

—H.H. Boyesen

This is not the place for a summary of Nordic immigrants' political participation in American politics. But to verify that they, and their descendants, did—readily—participate, a single example will be sufficient. In this writer's home state, Minnesota, from 1890 to the present day, most governors have had Nordic roots. Two of these whose statues stand guard in front of the state capital are Norwegian immigrant Knute Nelson (1892–1895) and Swedish immigrant John A. Johnson (1905–1909).

A Long-term Nordic Value: All have a voice; laws and institutions are necessary; justice rules.

11
Leaders in Progress

Chapter Two suggested that Nordic countries were in the past leaders in literacy and today are world leaders in many aspects of progress. "World leaders" refers to a country's ranking on progress indexes compiled by various organizations. These indexes rank nations in areas such as: do citizens have full political rights, do they have access to education, do they have access to quality health care, do they have the necessities of life, and so on. The table below summarizes six well-publicized indexes:

(A) The "Legatum Prosperity Index 2011" is published by the Legatum Institute in London. It attempts to measure factors that influence prosperity and includes detailed information for 110 countries.

(B) The "Human Development Index 2011" is published by the United Nations, who has been gathering data on a wide range of factors for thirty years. The 2011 index covers 187 countries.

(C) "Voice and Accountability 2010" is one of several "governance" indexes published by The World Bank. This organization, founded in 1944, is headquartered in Washington, D.C. and is owned by its member countries. "Voice and Accountability" measures how effectively citizens can influence their own government. It is often taken as a measure of corruption in government. The lower the rank, the more corrupt the government. The index covers 213 countries.

(D) The "Commitment to Development Index 2011" is published by the Center for Global Development, a nonprofit organization headquartered in Washington, D.C. As the name implies, this index measures ways in which the world's twenty-two richest nations assist poorer nations.

(E) "Global Gender Gap Report 2011" is one of several reports published by the World Economic Forum, an international organization that holds it annual meetings in Davos, Switzerland. These meetings include important government officials and business and industry leaders, as well as civic leaders. The gender gap report covers 135 countries.

(F) "Global Competitiveness Report 2011–2012" is published by the World Economic Forum (above). It covers 142 countries.

Relative Rankings of 20 European & "English-Speaking" Countries

Country   Index

	A	B	C	D	E	F
Norway	1	1	1	2	2	11
Sweden	5	8	3	1	4	2
Denmark	2	11	4	3	6	7
Finland	7	14	5	6	3	3
Netherlands	9	3	7	4	10	6
New Zealand	4	5	6	7	5	14
Switzerland	8	9	2	14	7	1
Australia	3	2	8	8	14	13
United States	10	4	15	5	12	4
Canada	6	6	11	10	13	9
Iceland	11	10	10	*	1	15
Germany	13	7	12	11	8	5
Belgium	14	12	9	12	9	10
UK	12	16	13	9	11	8
France	15	13	14	13	16	12
Italy	16	15	16	16	19	16
Hungary	17	18	17	*	20	17
Greece	18	17	18	15	17	20
Romania	19	19	19	*	18	19
Russian Fed.	20	20	20	*	15	18

* Not one of the twenty-two richest countries

On this chart, countries are ranked—arbitrarily—by their cumulative score. In case of a tie, the Prosperity Index (Index A) was used as a tiebreaker. Throughout these pages, the comparisons have been between Nordic and other European countries, but the United States and Canada were added because most readers would be curious about their ranking. Australia, New Zealand, and the UK were added because, together with the United States and Canada, they are sometimes lumped together by academic writers under the heading "English speaking" or "Anglo Saxon" countries.[314]

These numbers are already dated as they are being entered. Readers may wish to access the most recent rankings on the Internet, but more than that, examine how the indexes are compiled, what data goes into them, and who supplies that data. National statistics are also available from the Organization for Economic Cooperation and Development (OECD), which is not a source for this chart but is referenced elsewhere in these pages.

If the above chart is confusing or if a reader desires additional assurance, the position of the Nordic countries among the nations of the world is clearly visible in Figures 1 and 2 of *Human Beliefs and Values* (2004) edited by Inglehart, Basanez, Diez-Medrano, Halman, and Luijkx.

A Nordic country ranked first in the world on five of the six indexes, and a Nordic country is ranked second in the world on the remaining index (Global Competitiveness). Based on these indexes, Nordic countries are world leaders in progress.[315] How is it possible for a group of small nations, way up north, to consistently rank near the top on these indexes? Some possible explanations are: the indexes are inaccurate, the Nordic countries are lucky to have good government, they have inspired business and labor leaders, they have more natural resources, they have a better religion, or it's their culture.

Inaccurate. All information should be questioned and viewed critically, but these indexes are put out by different organizations, with different missions, and the relative position of the Nordic countries is fairly consistent. Probably, these well-publicized indexes are reasonably accurate.

Good Government. The various Nordic social welfare programs are part of the reason that Nordic countries rank high on world indexes, but politicians and government are downstream from culture.[316] You get what you deserve in politics. People's culture determines which politicians they vote for, and those politicians will govern based on their culture. Nordic social welfare programs, paid for by high taxes, are a fruit of shared culture.

Inspired Business and Labor Leaders. As with politicians, business and labor leaders are defined by culture (their actions and decisions reflect the attitudes and values of their culture).

Abundant Natural Resources. Norway has large oil reserves, and for several decades it has been a major exporter of oil. However, as this is a recent development, likely it is not a significant factor in the above indexes.[317] Otherwise, as they always have been, the Nordic countries are resource deficient.

Religion, the Protestant Ethic. A glance at the chart above makes it easy to understand why people believed that religion played a major role. The highest-ranking countries are predominantly Protestant, and the bottom-ranking countries are, or formerly were, predominantly Catholic or Orthodox. A Protestant Ethic appears to fit. But, in the Nordic region, religion never became entangled in laws, institutions, and everyday life to the extent that it did elsewhere.[318] And for the past half century only a fraction of Nordic people have routinely attended church. Religion is not a reasonable explanation for the success of Nordic peoples.

Long-Held Nordic Culture. Present-day society is enriched by individuals, both men and women, who take responsibility for themselves and who are accustomed to making decisions (Chapters Three and Four). Past efforts by parents to educate children for a variety of responsibilities (Chapter Five) have evolved into making education through the college level accessible to all. Group identity (mutual responsibilities, Chapter Seven) has created state systems that provide social services that in the past were provided by a family or a village. An ancient attitude toward authority with a strong emphasis on law, institutions, and justice (Chapter Ten), together with practical thinking (Chapter Nine) have created modern governments, responsive to the people, that focus on long-term solutions.

Because of culture, Nordic economies are nonideological mixtures of private property, individual initiative, government leadership, government ownership, and civic organizations' influence. People, businesses, industries, governments, and civic organizations are the reason that Nordic countries rank near the top of progress indexes. It is all based on culture.

As briefly mentioned earlier, equality has been credited with reducing personal initiative.[319] One is not supposed to stand above the group, and that no doubt reduces individual initiative. And, it is generally believed that social programs (a safety net) reduce individual initiative.

But economically stressed individuals are not in a position to take chances. Some level of security is necessary to have the luxury of trying something new. For example, Thomas Edison was wealthy enough to hire many people to help him with his experiments. Would Edison have invented a lightbulb if he needed to spend all of his time earning a living and was unable to hire anyone? Computers and related technology, the hallmark of our era, grew out of government-financed research for military weapons programs. Present-day research projects often require a group effort.

Because Nordic children became independent at an early age, they were forced to take the initiative to support themselves. Unlike their neighbors, in the past Nordic people were not really settled. To make a living, they often exploited a number of resources, some of which were far from home. They were accustomed to traveling and they needed a variety of skills. More than other Europeans, they could learn from people outside their home district. This may have encouraged initiative and innovation.[320]

The endless Nordic waterways, when they were not frozen, were a barrier to travel: they were challenging. The scarcity of good farmland and of other resources, as well as large (sometimes menacing) neighbors, were challenges. Challenges, which are possible to overcome, create innovation.[321] Nordic people did, and still do, respond to the challenges posed by their environment.

Chapter Two included a literacy chart for military conscripts from the late 1800s for fourteen European countries.[322] Literacy was, in the 1800s, a measure of progress, and it remains one today. If we combine the rankings from the 1800s' literacy chart ("L" below) with the *relative* rankings of those countries today on various progress indexes (listed above), it looks like this:

Country	L	A	B	C	D	E	F
Sweden	1	3	4	3	1	3	2
Norway	--	1	1	1	2	2	11
Germany	2	7	3	8	6	6	4
Denmark	3	2	6	4	3	4	6
Switzer.	4	5	5	2	9	5	1
Nether.	5	6	2	6	4	8	5
Finland	5	4	9	5	5	1	3
France	7	9	8	9	8	10	8
Belgium	8	8	7	7	7	7	7
Hungary**	9	11	12	11	*	14	10
Greece	10	12	11	12	10	11	14
Italy	11	10	10	10	11	13	9
Russia	12	14	14	14	*	9	12
Romania	13	13	13	13	*	12	13

* Not one of the twenty-two richest countries.

** On the present-day indexes, Hungary was substituted for Austria-Hungary on the old literacy chart. Serbia was omitted because it only recently again became an independent country.

Norway was not listed on the conscript literacy chart, but is here ranked according to the modern indexes. On present-day progress indexes Germany ranks significantly lower than it did on the old literacy chart, probably because East Germany was dominated by Communism for half a century.[323] And Italy has moved up two notches; otherwise, the relationship between these countries is similar today to what it was more than a century ago. The Nordic countries together with Switzerland and Netherlands are at the top, while Greece, Russia, and Romania rank lowest.

Mass emigration, World War I, the Russian Revolution, the rise of Communism, the Great Depression, World War II, incredible advances in technology, the fall of Communism, and innumerable changes in political parties and governments took place between the time of the literacy chart and the present-day rankings. But the *relationship* between these countries is almost stationary. Can this be explained by anything other than culture?

A few authorities refuse to believe that something as obscure and slippery as culture could really be important. But, the conclusions of this book are not new or unique; it is generally accepted that Nordic countries are progressive (rank high on progress indexes) because of their culture.[324] To examine that issue any further would be beating a dead horse—readers already know what they believe.

Twelve centuries ago, Viking ships were home-grown and practical. Using home-grown materials and home-grown skills, artisans created attractive and practical ships. These ships were capable of sailing into rivers and into shallow bays; they could be rowed or sailed; they were light enough to be pulled up unto a beach, and these ships could and did sail the oceans. Viking ships carried thousands of people and their property to Iceland in the 800s, and more than a thousand years ago Viking ships carried Nordic people to North America. These ships worked as they were intended to because Nordic people had been using ships for millennia. Viking ship design was the end result of many centuries of trial and error—what works best.

Today, Nordic governments and economies are home-grown and practical. Nordic democracies are among the most transparent and most corruption-free in the world. About 40 percent of elected legislators are women, and it is common for Nordic prime ministers to be women. Nordic countries are leaders in education, environmental science, urban planning, and efficient use of energy. Nordic companies excel in industries such as information technology, green technology, ocean shipping, high-tech machinery, and others. Today, Nordic countries export highly educated people.

12

American Culture

Up to this point Nordic culture has been explored by contrasting it with non-Nordic areas of Europe, with only brief references to America. But, our exploration of Nordic culture would be incomplete if it was not compared with American culture—"American" in this and later chapters refers to the United States. Canadians have their own culture, which is often imagined to be somewhere between United States and European cultures.[325]

Here, our exploration of Canadian culture will be limited to a single personal anecdote. In the days leading up to the U.S. invasion of Iraq, this writer was fortunate to enjoy morning coffee with a retired contractor from Saskatchewan, "John," who spent his winters in Arizona. We discussed the impending U.S. invasion and news reports relating to it. American news, especially TV, was full of stories about "shock and awe," advanced military technology, and WMDs (weapons of mass destruction). Except for editorials in the *Arizona Republic*, no news report that this writer saw questioned whether this war would be a good thing for the American people.

Over coffee, I said that Americans were not well served by this type of "news" and John agreed. Born in the Netherlands, John immigrated to Canada at age twenty under a program where he was required to work one year on a dairy farm. He did his one-year stint, moved on, and became a contractor in Saskatchewan. Because no one else in his birth family emigrated, John returned to Europe twenty times during fifty years. He believed that news in the United States was primarily entertainment, news in Europe was usually informative, and news in Canada was halfway between.

In Chapter One, readers were asked to remember that everyone is not the same: culture varies from individual to individual, and also from area to area. That applies to American culture as well; for example, on measures of progress (education, social mobility, health care, infant mortality, income inequality, and women's rights) there are significant differences between states.[326] Some (generally northern) states such as California, Colorado, Connecticut, Iowa, Kansas, Massachusetts, Minnesota, North Dakota, New Hampshire, Oregon, Utah, Vermont, Washington, and Wisconsin consistently rank higher than the nation as a whole.

And, we are almost evenly divided politically, with culture partly responsible for that divide. So, to facilitate comparison, a cross-section of American culture was adopted that sharpens the contrast with Nordic culture, and which this writer believes is more or less accurate for Americans generally. It certainly doesn't fit everyone.

126

The table below is a possible framework for thinking about the contrasts between American and Nordic cultures:

American Culture	Nordic Culture
Individualism	**Group Identity**
Private property	Private property, less rights
Women's rights	Gender equality
Competition/adversarial	Cooperation/consensus
Ambition, hard work	Mutual responsibilities
Education is important	Civic organizations
Stand above, celebrity	Equality in education
Conspicuous waste	Achievement (Nobel Prizes)
	Social pressure, *lagom*
Ideologies	**Practical Thinking**
Absolute, bad or good	What works best
Religion	Religion separate
Adam Smith, Ayn Rand	Government leadership
Free-market capitalism	Private-public blend
Entertaining news	Informative news
Inspiring stories	Careful analysis
Political spin	Truth-telling
Equal opportunity	Equality of outcome

In 1890s' America, when "European" meant "immigrant," Harvard historian Frederick Jackson Turner theorized that a centuries-long (as settlement slowly expanded west) frontier environment was critical to the triumph of American over "European" culture. A later Danish-American writer embellished Turner's theory by contrasting paternalistic German immigrants with speculative Americans.[327] The German wanted to establish a patriarchy based on land (sacred and not for sale) while the clever Yankee thought of land as a source of profit and was always ready to sell and move to greener pastures. In this contrast "German" was, with sketchy evidence, expanded into "European."

> [Yankee farmers] would willingly part [with their land] if they scented a speculative gain.[328]

> —*Marcus Lee Hansen*

However accurate this argument was for German immigrants, it doesn't fit when comparing Nordic and American culture. Scandinavian immigrants (with few exceptions) had nuclear families, independent women, and children who became independent at an early age—they were not paternalistic, and they were mobile.[329] And, regardless of how attractive it is to trace our American culture to the frontier, and although "rugged individualism" was clearly visible there, American frontier culture was most likely well-rooted in earlier attitudes and values.[330]

To this day, differences between "European" (non-Nordic) culture and American culture are sometimes attributed to the fact that Americans never experienced feudalism.[331] That may be true, but Black Americans experienced slavery, which was worse than feudalism, and besides, most of the Nordic region never experienced feudalism. This explanation is not valid here.

Preconceived notions about the differences between European and American culture could hinder an understanding of the differences outlined below.

Some Americans might assume that the Nordic countries are socialist, and that "socialism" means public ownership. Nordic governments often refer to themselves as "socialist" but that generally implies a social safety net of government programs that benefit people, such as Medicare and Medicaid in the United States. Centuries ago, in most of the Nordic region, people owned their homes, livestock, and fields, and today most Nordic businesses are privately owned.

Private property is a fundamental aspiration for Americans. We own—or we would like to own—homes, vacation homes, automobiles, all types of recreational toys, businesses, land, stocks, bonds, mutual funds, bank accounts, gold, etc. Most of us, without thinking, assume that our ownership is absolute, but it is not. We accept zoning; probably (outside of Nevada) one wouldn't be allowed to establish a brothel or start a nuclear waste dump. Our automobiles have to have safety equipment, they have to be used properly and they need to be licensed. If we own rental property, we must comply with certain rules. And so on. Americans accept, sometimes grudgingly, restrictions on their property rights. And there is public property in the United States, including huge areas of government-owned land (national parks and other land).

Private property is an ancient tradition for Nordic people, but there are restrictions. Laws in Nordic countries allow the public to use the countryside (private property) to bike, hike, swim, harvest berries and mushrooms, and camp briefly—as long as one does no damage.[332] Forest regulations require Nordic landowners to plant certain trees, eliminate detrimental trees, harvest at a certain time, and so forth. The land is privately owned, but forests are a vital national resource, and they are managed as such.

American farmers (at least in the past) who participated in government farm programs were restricted as to what or how much they could plant. But the farmer was (if he or she didn't need the money) participating voluntarily, while the Nordic forest owner is not. In some gated communities, wealthy Americans may be restricted as to what type of home they build, what color they paint it, where they park their car, and what kind of shrubs or trees they plant, but these restrictions do not come from a state or national government.

In the United States it is assumed that businesses are privately owned. From the smallest boutique to a giant multinational corporation, businesses are supposed to be private not public. Actually, there are significant exceptions (cooperative utilities, nonprofits, businesses that depend on government, etc.), but the exceptions don't change Americans' assumption that businesses are supposed to be private.

In some circumstances, Nordic people assume that public (government-owned) businesses are natural and desirable. Businesses such as utilities might be 100 percent state-owned, or a business might be both privately owned and state-owned. One example of this is Statoil (STO on the New York Stock Exchange), which is a large international oil and gas company. Statoil stock is about one-third privately owned and about two-thirds owned by the Norwegian government. And besides, Norway's offshore oil reserves are considered a national treasure: it is natural that Norwegians should benefit from exploiting those reserves.

In summary, private property is the rule among both Americans and Nordic people, but Nordic people accept more restrictions on their property rights (and benefit accordingly), and Nordic people accept state participation in business and industry, which is about 90 percent private.

As Americans we see ourselves as, and we view others as, individuals, but more than that, we assume that personal ambition and hard work are natural and desirable for each of us. We expect ourselves and others to be competitive. We are naturally competitive in everyday conversations, dating, playing games, participating in athletics, religion, school, status (accumulating wealth), at work—everywhere. "May the best man win."

Our cultural expectations just naturally produce an explanation of individual success. Success (winning) is achieved by hard work, ambition, and vigorous competition; conversely, those who fail (lose) are lacking in one or more of our expectations.[333] Often, because people are responsible for their own failure, we ignore them. The instant an athletic event is decided, the TV camera focuses on the winner and neglects the loser. We admire winners, look up to winners, and emulate winners—but not losers.

Competition has a goal. We are competing individually, and often there is a tangible goal: friendship, a desirable mate, an athletic medal, praise, publicity, a good education, a good job, or status. For Americans, "status" is not far removed from money. Money buys status; if any reader doubts that, try to visualize "keeping up with the Joneses" without money.

[T]he American . . . is individual centered . . . Money is the measure of success.[334]

—*E. Adamson Hoebel*

131

Competition is subject to rules. If you win a game by cheating, then you are not a winner. You are expected to follow good sportsmanship in athletic events. Among friends, there might be limits on competition. Americans interact with businesses constantly and they, like individuals, are expected to compete within rules. But what are the rules? Is not breaking any laws enough, or are there other rules (values) that businesses and individuals are expected to observe?[335]

Research by Rushford Kidder identified five values that are common (but not universal) across cultures and across time: respect, honesty, compassion, fairness, and responsibility.[336] Presumably, if they were asked, many Americans would agree that these five values should be observed by individuals and businesses.

But, in our American culture where ambition, competition, and individualism are encouraged, and where success is measured in money, these values (ethics) may be seen as obstacles to be circumvented or ignored. With individualism, adherence to ethical values is altruistic; individuals or businesses that adhere to these values would, from time to time, lose a competitive advantage and be acting against their own self-interest.[337]

This conflict between our culture and commonly accepted values might, to some degree, explain why teaching ethical values is not a high priority in American schools.[338] For example, a local (Minnesota) high school has a large poster on a lobby wall with this wording: "We expect: Honesty, Respect, Self-discipline, Responsibility, Compassion." Other nearby schools have similar posters but not always with the same principles. One might imagine that these posters are a response to discipline problems, and that values are not taught in the same way—to the same extent—that reading or math or science is taught. And when business school students study ethics, it may serve to make them more proficient at rationalizing unethical practices.[339]

Because of the high value we place on competition, it is not surprising that none of the school posters included "cooperation" as a principle.[340] But cooperation is fundamental to Nordic culture, and Nordic schools teach principles.[341] But, whatever the role of teaching, transmitting and observing ethical values is usually subconscious.[342]

Because values—in the form of mutual responsibilities—are a priority for Nordic people, laws regulating businesses may be less necessary in the Nordic countries than they are in the United States with our competitive individualism and free-market economy.[343]

In the Nordic countries, athletic competition between individuals and between countries is intense. For example, years ago when Finland and Sweden met in an Olympic hockey match, 70 percent of the population of both countries watched on TV—they are competitive. As in athletics, Nordic countries compete vigorously in measures of "Progress" as expressed in the international indexes mentioned repeatedly in these pages. And each of the Nordic countries is economically dependent on exports; most Nordic businesses must be globally competitive to survive.

Nordic individual achievement is applauded. Grundtvig, Sibelius, Snorri, Nansen, and Linnaeus are remembered and celebrated for their individual achievements. Individual achievement was and is part of Nordic culture, but here "achievement" means accomplishing something valued by Nordic culture. Being richer or more successful in business, standing above others, might make a person well-known, but it is not celebrated in the Nordic countries.

Regardless of any assumed contradictions, parallel with competition and individual achievement, Nordic people are members of a group (Chapter Seven). They have mutual responsibilities to each other such as fairness and justice, respect, honesty and truth-telling, cooperation, etc. These mutual responsibilities are as natural for Nordic people as rugged individualism and pursuing status (money) are natural for Americans.

> [Political] parties in Finland tend to be quite similar and harmonious.[344]
>
> *—Finnish American Reporter*

Because cooperation is natural and expected, Nordic government is different; generally politicians treat each other with respect, and they cooperate with each other.[345] This "harmonious" government is often attributed to the parliamentary system with shifting alliances among numerous political parties. A more likely explanation is that Nordic governments reflect Nordic culture—cooperative, tolerant, and respectful.

> Swedish life in general and politics particularly should be LAGOM . . . acceptable to everyone.[346]
>
> *—Ulf Nilsson in* Nordstjernan

In summary, Nordic people might be characterized as

having a group identity (mutual responsibilities) and an appreciation for culturally valued achievement. Americans might be characterized as individualistic and competitive with success measured in money. These characterizations are simple generalizations and, as always, there are exceptions.

Americans place a high value on education. Politicians propose and debate different programs for improving education; schools actively compete for students; teachers are praised or criticized; parents compete to have their children accepted by desirable schools. Almost daily, our media reports on new developments in education.

We are individuals who believe in competition, so it is natural that we test and grade students, and student test results can be used to evaluate teachers as well as to grade and rank schools. Students, teachers, and schools are all competing. With all of the interest in education and all of the competition, one might well imagine that America is a world leader in education.

Education is integral to American values (ideology)— education is necessary to be successful. But our values also include individualism and equal opportunity; children should have opportunity, access to quality education—it is up to each of them to take advantage of that opportunity.

If anything, Nordic people place a higher value on education than Americans, but a more significant difference is a holistic approach with an emphasis on actual equality rather than opportunity. Equality is fundamental in Nordic schools.[347]

Nordic people use practical thinking and—apparently—Americans use ideologies (or an ideology). Defined by its customary effect, in these pages "ideology" has a specific meaning: *An ideology frees its believer from practical thinking.* Here, an ideology may be one belief or several; it may be secular or religious. The single qualification is that it frees a believer from thinking.[348]

Ideology is just an escape from thinking.

—*John Kenneth Galbraith*

Often, ideologies encourage believers to think in ideal terms, black and white or good and evil, and one of the questions (F022) asked on the *Human Beliefs and Values* surveys (2004) measured this. Those who thought in terms of good and evil were: United States 49 percent, Canada 42 percent, Australia 42 percent, New Zealand 42 percent, Great Britain 42 percent, Russia 39 percent, Italy 36 percent, Germany 35 percent, Finland 29 percent, Norway 29 percent, Switzerland 28 percent, Netherlands 27 percent, France 25 percent, Sweden 16 percent, Denmark 10 percent, and Iceland 9 percent.[349] About one half of Americans view life in terms of good and evil; on average, about one-fifth of Nordic people see it that way.

Thinking in terms of good and evil was typical in feudal Europe eight hundred years ago. At that time, "history" consisted of stories that contained a grain of truth around which an ideal story had been fabricated. Heroes were pure, their cause was just, and their enemies were evil.[350] In terms of black and white, there are no nuances, no messy details or extenuating circumstances (there is no need to think). Thinking usually produces shades of gray rather than black and white.

It has been our fate as a nation not to have ideologies, but to be one.[351]

—Richard Hofstadter

It is a common notion that being an American presupposes an ideology.[352] Citizens of other nations share a long history while Americans share an ideology. We believe in freedom, individualism, competition, democracy, value of hard work and education, patriotism, private enterprise, and so on. Part of our inherent ideology is referred to as the "free market."

The free market is both an ideal and a long-accepted ideology; a century or more ago it was pretty well covered by "laissez-faire" (hands off business). And nineteenth-century Americans were acquainted with ideals:

> [*Idealism*] gave to the pioneer farmer and city builder a restless energy, a quick capacity for judgment and action, a belief in liberty, freedom of opportunity, and a resistance to the domination of class . . .[353]

—Frederick Jackson Turner

Ideally, individuals and businesses, pursuing their own interests—unencumbered by government regulations—will produce the most good for the most people.[354] Private interests and actions are good; government interference is evil. For example, a former chairman of the Federal Reserve, Alan Greenspan, believed that laws against fraud by securities dealers were unnecessary because customers would find out if a broker was dishonest and they would take their business elsewhere.[355] *Ideally* the system (free market) would operate without laws (government interference). Naturally, under Greenspan's leadership, it was not necessary for the Fed to enforce regulations against deceptive mortgage practices.[356]

Greenspan believed in free-market ideology, and he was a long-time associate of Ayn Rand who wrote *Atlas Shrugged* (1957).[357] Read by tens of millions of Americans, *Atlas Shrugged* may be one of the most influential books ever published in the United States.[358] Its theme is that each person should pursue his or her own selfish goals and that it is wrong to sacrifice for others.[359] Rand idealized selfishness. Her philosophy is consistent with free-market ideology, and she was an idealist.

Selfishness is visible in the writing of English political economist Adam Smith (1723–1790) whose *Wealth of Nations* is the bedrock of free-market ideology:

> It is not from benevolence of the butcher, the brewer, or the baker that we expect our dinner, but from their regard to their own self-interest. We address ourselves, not to their humanity, but to their self-love.[360]

Smith's writing is free-market ideology. The greatest good for the greatest number will come—without government interference—from each person (or company) pursuing selfish motives.

> Anybody has a right to evade taxes if he can get away with it. No citizen has a moral obligation to assist in maintaining the government.
>
> —*J.P. Morgan*

The writing of economist Milton Friedman, as it applies to American business, is consistent with a free market. In "The Social Responsibility of Business Is to Increase Its Profits," he argued that business executives' sole responsibility is to shareholders.[361] For Friedman, the free market was an *ideal*; increasing shareholder profits was good, business expenditures which benefited the public were wrong (evil).

If the free market is an ideal—if it is an ideology—then by the previously stated definition it should free its believers from practical thinking. And it does. For example, as outlined above, the philosophy of Adam Smith is a pillar of free-market ideology. But Adam Smith had much more to say, including:

> The wise and virtuous man is at all times willing that his own private interest should be sacrificed to the public interest . . .[362]

This quote, and much of Adam Smith's writing, is not consistent with free-market ideology.[363]

Advocates of free-market ideology have used excerpts from Adam Smith while they ignore anything he wrote that contradicts their ideology. Using excerpts while ignoring other information is accepted in some situations; this can be seen, for example, with the ancient Greeks, where it is not unusual to find a valuable insight hidden among heaps of philosophical rubbish.[364] But that does not apply to the writing of Adam Smith, whose insight appears quite uniform throughout his writing. Proponents of free-market ideology who quote Adam Smith are choosing evidence.

Feel-good stories may be another example of choosing evidence. This writer recently attended a presentation by the CEO of one of America's largest banks. The CEO mentioned briefly that he was from a large, rural family; he was proof that the American dream works. Practical thinking on this subject would require one to examine evidence of social mobility (next chapter). One instance is an example that an ideology works, but someone thinking about this subject would want more information than just a single example.

A recent TV news program, viewed by this writer, focused on a homeless teenage girl who was excelling in school. By anyone's standards, she was an outstanding student, and because of her ability will, no doubt, be offered a full scholarship to college. This is an example that the American dream is alive and well. But, practical thinking would require exploring information about the overwhelming majority of homeless students who would benefit from having a home and a stable life.

Choosing evidence is visible in the "natural" justification for free-market ideology. People are not naturally altruistic (it goes against their genes), and they are naturally selfish so free-market ideology (based on selfishness) is natural; any restrictions on selfishness amount to altruism, which is unnatural. But selfishness versus altruism is a false comparison (apples versus oranges). A valid comparison would involve selfishness, empathy, fairness and justice, and cooperation.

Most readers have witnessed enough selfish behavior to assume that it is natural, but empathy is also natural. Studies of baby girls have found that they are hardwired for empathy.[365] Perhaps, girls are more empathetic, boys are more selfish, and our society chooses to ignore what is natural for girls. But empathy may not be exclusively human. Observations of primates and laboratory experiments with rats have produced strong evidence of natural hardwired empathy in animals.[366] Probably, empathy is a natural human trait, and Adam Smith (apparently) didn't believe that it was restricted by gender. He believed that if a man witnessed someone else being injured, he would naturally react as if he felt, to some degree, the other person's pain.[367]

If we are naturally selfish, we also have a natural affinity for fairness and justice.[368] It isn't necessary to teach a child that she deserves as large a portion of a desirable treat as others, or that he should be allowed to participate in a fun activity with others.

And we are natural, hardwired cooperators.[369] We would not be here if our ancestors, for untold generations, had not cooperated at the level of family and community.[370] The question is not whether we naturally cooperate, but rather: what is the radius of our cooperation? Per Albin Hansson, Swedish Prime Minister from 1932 to 1946, believed that the radius could be expanded from the home (which is generally accepted) to include all citizens.[371]

Thousands of instances are known where groups of ordinary people have devised centuries-long strategies for sharing resources—cooperatively.[372] There is nothing altruistic about these strategies. They are hardheaded (carefully thought out), and they include sanctions if people do not do their share of the work or if they take more than their share, they include establishing limits to avoid depleting the resource, and so on. These bottom-up complex strategies to cooperatively exploit resources appear to have one limitation: the participants must be nearly equal.

And, as mentioned elsewhere, we may be hardwired for something, but experience and environment (culture) can rewire us (to some extent at least). Free-market ideology's focus on selfishness is an example of choosing evidence because alternatively, empathy, a sense of fairness and justice, and cooperation are just as natural.

In summary, often ideologies free Americans from practical thinking; choosing evidence and isolated examples provide adequate proof (that is not true in the Nordic countries). If a free market was not an ideology, we would be free to think about it. We could use and respect it where appropriate, regulate it when that was desirable, and use other methods where a free market would be harmful, all without tribulation—if the free market was not an ideology.[373]

> Democracy is when the indigent, and not the men of power, are the rulers.
>
> —*Aristotle*

The United States began as an egalitarian democracy (one person, one vote), and we rejected the verbal and physical deference that was long customary for Europeans; it would be easy to assume that our attitude toward authority was similar to—or more advanced than—the Nordic countries. That may not be true.

The idealism of Enlightenment writers that found its way into our Declaration of Independence and into our Constitution was not an everyday reality. For example,

Jefferson wrote that "all men are created equal," but he himself owned more than a hundred slaves. In the early decades of the United States only land-owning White men were allowed to vote; before 1820, fewer than 5 percent of the population usually voted.[374] After the Civil War, Black men could vote, but that didn't last long. Native Americans and women were not allowed to vote nationally until the twentieth century. In the southern United States, Black men and women were not allowed to vote in significant numbers until the 1960s. "One person, one vote" (bottom-up authority) has gradually become a reality only within the last century.

Americans did reject physical and verbal deference, but we began as English colonies and we may have inherited an English attitude toward authority.[375] The English were and are proud of their aristocracy and their royalty. That is not true for Americans: we have no official aristocracy and no royalty, but our founding fathers were, generally, aristocrats. And today, we may have substituted a much richer upper class for an aristocracy, and we may have substituted "celebrity" for royalty. There is a reasonable argument for equating large income differences with status—much richer is, in many ways, equivalent to being aristocratic.[376] To the extent that some Americans believe they are entitled to much greater wealth, and to use that wealth to protect and enhance a privileged position, they are, in effect, aristocrats.

Aristocrats deserve more authority than ordinary people; if Americans accept an aristocracy (a much richer upper class) it should show up in our attitude toward authority. Apparently it does—question E114A on the *Human Beliefs and Values* surveys is evidence of peoples' attitude toward authority: It is a good idea to have a strong leader who is not hindered by congress or elections? The yes answers were: Romania 67 percent, Russia 49 percent, France 35 percent, Belgium 33 percent, Switzerland 31, United States 30 percent, Netherlands 27 percent, Finland 27 percent, Australia 25 percent, UK 25 percent, Canada 23 percent, Sweden 22 percent, New Zealand 19 percent, Germany 16 percent, Italy 16 percent, Denmark 14 percent, Norway 14 percent, Iceland 11 percent, and Greece 9 percent.

On this question, on average, 50 percent more Americans approve of top-down authority than is true for Nordic people, but question E114A is extreme—it represents a rejection of democracy. Probably, the differences between Americans and Nordic people related to deferring to (or obeying) authority are greater than their differences in answering this question.

Two values contribute to the different Nordic attitude: independent children and a more equal society. In an equal society, where authority belongs to the people, obedience (or deference) to authority is a nonissue. People observe cultural values (law-abiding, respect, etc.), but there is no higher authority to obey—obedience to authority is related to hierarchy (inequality).[377] And Emmanuel Todd was correct: nuclear families (independent children) are related to democracy (bottom-up authority).

Obedience to authority was visible at the Winter Olympics in 1936, which were held in Nazi Germany. There, winning athletes were instructed to salute Hitler when they received their medal, but Vivi-Anne Hulten, winner of the Bronze Medal in figure skating, refused:

I told them, I'm Swedish; I don't do that. . . I just stared at him.[378]

Obedience to authority was the subject of multiple experiments by Stanley Milgram of Yale University in the 1960s. The disturbing results of these experiments showed that twenty-six out of forty Americans would administer painful, possibly fatal electrical shocks to another person if ordered to do so by a man in a white lab coat.[379] There is some criticism, but Milgram's experiments are often quoted, and his results are accepted. And, for present-day Americans, if authority implies hierarchy, then our acceptance of a de facto aristocracy (a much richer upper class) suggests that we accept top-down authority.

Unless Milgram's obedience experiment was replicated in a Nordic country (this writer was unable to find that), no direct American-to-Nordic comparison is possible. But, Milgram's experiment was inspired by the Nazi's obedience to authority, and there is an example of Nordic (Danish) obedience to Nazi authority. After they were invaded and occupied, Danes attempted to adjust to (make the best of) this difficult situation, but that changed when the Nazis ordered that all Danish Jews be rounded up so they could be sent to concentration camps. Risking their lives, Danes saved their Jewish neighbors by rowing them (under cover of darkness) in small boats to Sweden. Reportedly, 98 percent of Danish Jews survived.[380]

A young Swede, Rauol Wallenberg, who studied architecture at the University of Michigan in the early 1930s, was surprised by American students' attitude toward authority. He observed that his fellow students expected, accepted, and trusted leadership (authority) from others. American students' attitude toward authority was directly opposite of students' attitude toward authority in Sweden.[381]

If Wallenberg's observation was accurate, is there a connection between trust in authority and America's low voter turnout? The eligible voters who voted in lower house congressional elections from 1960 to 1995 were: Iceland 89 percent, Denmark 87 percent, Sweden 86 percent, Norway 81 percent, and Finland 78 percent versus the United States with only 48 percent.[382] Is it possible that one of every two Americans accepts (or trusts in) top-down authority? A much higher percentage of Americans are religious than is true in the Nordic countries, and deference to religious authority is related to deference to political authority— naturally, Americans would be more accepting of top-down authority.[383]

On the other hand, maybe some voters don't vote because they believe that government does not work for them. To the extent that government does not reflect the interests of the majority of voters, the situation bears some resemblance to the late feudal era when laws and institutions were established but the real authority continued to be top-down. If government actions (or inaction) favored wealthy individuals and big businesses to the detriment of ordinary voters, would that be evidence of top-down authority?[384]

A simple example of how this relates to culture is appropriate here. If a banking executive acquiesced in and profited from actions that ultimately forced thousands of families out of their homes, what would happen to him? If a banking executive molested a five-year-old boy, what would happen to him? We do not accept molesting children, but, apparently, we accept top-down authority, and we accept that economic exploitation is natural in a free-market economy. That's culture.

Compared to the Nordic countries, Americans have a less equal society, we are more likely to accept top-down authority, and we are more prone to defer to (obey) authority.

13

Consequences

The previous chapter contrasted American and Nordic cultures, and this chapter focuses on the consequences of culture. In the following pages, some readers will wonder how it is possible to ignore laws and politics. As mentioned earlier, here the perspective is (assuming leaders and the general population share the same culture) that laws and politics are downstream from culture.[385] Laws and how they are enforced (or not) reflect society's attitudes and values.

[Laws] do not fall from the sky; they reflect the prevailing norms and mores of the wider society.[386]

—John Calvert

In some traditional societies, men expend considerable time and effort keeping women in their—unequal—place, and among the rich nations there is considerable variation in the status of women. The United States is a world leader in women's rights, and, generally, we now include women in our value of equal opportunity; women should be able to advance or excel in politics, business, athletics, and so on.

The *Human Beliefs and Values* (2004) surveys contains a question that confirms our role near the top in granting equal opportunity to women: Question C001 asks if men should be given priority when there is a shortage of jobs? The United States together with the Nordic countries, Netherlands, New Zealand, Estonia, and Canada strongly rejected that concept. We believe in equal opportunity.

The Nordic approach is not equal opportunity, it is equality—gender equality. The Global Gender Gap Report includes a ranking of countries by the percentage of women in the lower house of parliament (congress). The relative ranking for 2011 (same countries as used in Chapter Eleven) are:

1 Sweden
2 Iceland
3 Finland
4 Norway
5 Netherlands
6 Belgium
7 Denmark
8 New Zealand
9 Germany
10 Switzerland
11 Canada
12 Australia
13 United Kingdom
14 Italy
15 France

16 Greece
17 United States
18 Romania
19 Russian Federation
20 Hungary

In recent years, Finland, Iceland, and Denmark have had women prime ministers (corresponding to our president).

[1930. In Finland it is] taken for granted that men and women are equal in all respects . . . no one even stops to think which sex is entitled to certain jobs.[387]

—*Harry A. Franck*

Readers may have heard reports that the distribution of income in America is more unequal than is true in other rich countries. The Nordic countries are on the other end of the scale with the least income inequality. The degree of income inequality in a society affects crime, education, obesity, physical and mental health, and social mobility (equal opportunity). That topic is explored in detail by British authors Richard Wilkinson and Kate Pickett in *The Spirit Level: Why Greater Equality Makes Societies Stronger.* Readers who are interested in this subject are encouraged to read Wilkinson and Pickett's book.

Part of our American ideology is equal opportunity, "life, liberty and the pursuit of happiness." As always, the Nordic approach is equality rather than equal opportunity. Through high taxes, social programs, and social pressure, Nordic countries have achieved societies that are much more equal than American society. And they have higher levels of "equal opportunity." Nordic individuals have more opportunity to rise above their parents' position in society than do Americans. A study sponsored by the London School of Economics, covering eight rich countries, found that the United States had the lowest social mobility while Norway, Sweden, Denmark, Canada, and Finland had the highest.[388]

Both place a high value on it, but Americans and Nordic people have different strategies for education. Often, Americans emphasize reading, math and science, longer hours, more years, testing and retesting, and competition at every level.

Nordic people imagine that learning begins at birth, and the first years are critical for babies and young children.[389] They need a warm supportive environment, and they need to bond with and interact with their parents. Typically, Nordic parents receive paid maternity leave—possibly a year for the mother and less than that for the father (their jobs are held open).[390] If both parents return to work, the child may attend a daycare where the workers have an advanced education in child development. When the child starts school, there is no grading and no testing until they are teenagers. Whenever possible, a teacher stays with the same group of students for about seven years.[391] Students are taught equality; they are also taught to respect others and to cooperate with them, but at the same time they are taught to stand up for themselves and for what is right.[392]

Probably, Nordic students are different from American students. Before they enter school, children have already absorbed culture; they reflect the parenting they have received, they reflect the society they have been raised in, and they reflect their parents' values.[393] More than one writer has commented on how well behaved Nordic children are.[394] And probably they are more receptive to learning.

Compared to Nordic students, American students are more diverse; we have more minority students, and we have an "achievement gap" that is associated with both minority students and poverty.[395] Researchers have noted differences in culture related to poverty; some poor people do not place a high value on education for their children, and do not encourage their children to be ambitious.[396] This different culture is associated in the United States with poor minorities, but a similar culture is found among poor people in the UK who are working-class Whites—they are not an ethnic minority.[397]

The active ingredient here appears to be high income inequality (relative poverty). Although their access to services and opportunities is inferior, poor people may have enough to eat and they may have TVs, sometimes even iPhones.[398] However, they are constantly aware that they are at the bottom of society, looked down on by everyone— they are alienated.

> [1930] Thanks partly to government assistance when it is needed, Danish laborers are better housed on the average than those in the United States. There are no slums in Copenhagen, no real poverty . . .[399]
>
> —*Harry A. Franck*

Associating poor performance in school (and other social ills) with income inequality fits the United States (high inequality and poor performance in education).[400] It also fits the Nordic countries that emphasize actual equality and who rank high on almost any measure of progress including education. And, an OECD study found that many countries are as diverse as the United States, but we are unique in the way socioeconomic disadvantage is linked to underachievement in academics.[401]

The 2009 results of the Program for International Student Assessment (PISA) provide a comparison of students' proficiency in reading, science, and math. American students ranked above average for OECD (rich) countries, fourteenth out of thirty-four, and they were ahead of Swedish and Danish students in reading. American students were average, seventeenth out of thirty-four, and ahead of Norwegian, Danish, and Swedish students in science. American students were below average, twenty-fifth out of thirty-four, and behind all of the Nordic students in math.[402]

If this were the whole story we could say that American education was average for these thirty-four rich nations, but it's not. For example, reading; students were tested in their first language, and Nordic students are generally proficient in two and sometimes three languages. How would American students compare with Nordic students if the reading test were in the students' second language? What about citizenship skills, history, and knowledge of foreign cultures that is necessary in a global economy?[403]

What about adult education? Since Danish pastor and educator N.F.S. Grundtvig (1783–1872) founded the first Folk High School, hundreds of these schools have been established in the Nordic countries. Thousands of study circles provide a genuine educational opportunity for millions of Nordic adults.[404]

[W]hen compared with Americans . . . [Norwegian students] value hard work rather than personality, they want to be independent rather than well-liked.[405]

—*Christen T. Jonassen*

And Nordic students are more practical; they are more likely to pursue an education in the hard sciences that are critical to a modern economy. For example, Nordic students are more than three times as likely as Americans to earn a doctorial degree in materials science and engineering.[406] But, this is not a fair comparison because the figure for Americans is inflated by a high number of foreign students who return to their homeland after graduation.

If the whole story could be told, American education does not compare well with Nordic education. This discussion of education is continued later in this chapter.

Americans are concerned about their health, and we spend 20 percent or more of our GDP on health care. This is more than other nations spend, and it must have a negative influence on companies who compete globally. Often, U.S. companies pay for some or most of their employees' health care insurance, while their foreign competition pays nothing because of national health care systems. But however it is paid, our large expenditures on health care (for example, two-and-one-half times Japan) put us at a competitive disadvantage globally.

But high cost and competitive disadvantage are nonissues because Americans believe that we have the best health care in the world. In 1950 the United States was a world leader in health, but that may no longer, generally, be true.[407] America still leads in treating some cancers, some states provide much better care than others, people come from all over the world to be treated at the Mayo Clinic, and the health care reform legislation of 2010 made health care available to tens of millions of uninsured Americans. This legislation apparently led to a top ranking in health care for the United States on the 2011 Legatum Prosperity Index (Chapter Eleven).

Health care is often measured in one of three ways: life expectancy, outcomes, and infant mortality. Infant mortality statistics are published by the Organization for Economic Cooperation and Development (OECD), which includes thirty-four rich nations. In 2008, the most recent year for which complete figures are available, the United States ranked thirty-first out of thirty-four OECD nations in infant mortality; Chile, Turkey, and Mexico had lower rankings.

"Outcomes" are the likelihood that a person who shows up at a health care provider and reports certain symptoms will be effectively treated. In spite of much higher spending, we do not rank above average compared with other OECD countries in health outcomes.[408]

A study published in the *Journal of the American Medical Association* in 2006 compared the rates of serious illnesses among middle-aged White men in the United States and England by education. In every case, the rate of illness was higher among Americans, and (except for cancer) the higher one's education, the lower the rate of illness. The conclusion was that English society was more equal and thus healthier.[409]

Another study compared the death rates of working-age men in England and Wales with their counterparts in Sweden, by social class. Deaths per 100,000 were significantly lower in Sweden regardless of class, but the largest difference was for those who had been put in the lowest class. Swedish men from the lowest class had a lower death rate than English and Welsh men from the highest class.[410]

Still another study compared infant mortality in England and Wales with infant mortality in Sweden.[411] The results mirrored the death rate study above and, for single mothers, the infant mortality rate was twice as high in England and Wales. But this "single mother" statistic is likely misleading because there is less pressure for couples to be married in Sweden.

The "State of the World's Mothers Report" published annually by the International Save the Children Alliance ranks countries on a number of elements including, but not limited to: maternity leave, educational opportunities for young children, and maternal deaths. The 2010 "Mother's Index" rankings for the countries listed in Chapter Eleven were:

1 Norway

2 Australia

3 Sweden

3 Iceland

5 Denmark

7 Finland

8 Netherlands

9 Germany

9 Belgium

12 France

14 United Kingdom

15 Switzerland

17 Italy

20 Canada

21 Hungary

24 Greece

28 United States

37 Romania

38 Russian Federation

New Zealand was listed on this index but it was not ranked. The maternal death rate is part of this index and according to the report, on average, during her lifetime a Nordic woman's likelihood of dying from maternity related causes was about one in 13,500 while the comparable ratio for the United States was one in 4,800—American women are 2.8 times more likely to die from maternity related causes. And it is safe to assume that the data from the Nordic countries is accurate.

Business ethics as it relates to both society and the environment is sometimes referred to by a special term, Corporate Social Responsibility (CSR).

[E]thics and social responsibility always have been an inherent [Nordic] way of doing business.[412]

—*Mette Morsing, Atle Midttun, Karl Palmås*

Nordic CEOs and workers have group identity with mutual responsibilities, which may explain their attitude toward CSR.[413] For example, rather than resisting pollution regulations, Nordic businesses are likely to be leaders on environmental issues. Business leadership may be partly responsible for the fact that Nordic countries have concrete programs in place to reduce their carbon footprint to zero.

One index of CSR (based on DJSI, FTSE4Good, and Global 100) found that Italy, the United States, Austria, and Greece rank low while Norway, Sweden, Denmark, Finland, and Netherlands rank high in corporate social responsibility.[414] For example, in 2012 a Danish health care company, Novo Nordisk, was ranked by the World Economic Forum at the top for sustainability.[415]

Ethics in business is not a new thing for Nordic people. Here is an upper-class Norwegian's advice to a younger man who wished to become a merchant, circa A.D. 1247:

> If they [goods purchased for resale] are found to be injured and you are about to dispose of them, do not conceal the flaws from the purchaser: show him what the defects are and make such a bargain as you can; then you cannot be called a deceiver.[416]

> —*The King's Mirror*

Business practices which suggest that some large American companies do not accept Corporate Social Responsibility include:

(1) A bank attempting to fool its customers with deceptive or misleading terms and conditions on credit cards or loan agreements.[417]

(2) A tobacco company whose marketing is really aimed at young people (attempting to addict new smokers).

(3) A pharmaceutical company that prices its drugs at all-the-traffic will bear (50 times cost?) thereby insuring that people without good insurance must do without their medicine.

These business practices occasionally cause someone to lose their health, or to lose their home, or even to lose their life, but—apparently—they do not violate American values (individualism, free market ideology, money equals success).[418]

"Robo-signing" is an example of a business practice that violated both CSR and American values (because it was illegal): In 2012 five of the largest American banks agreed to a $25 billion settlement for "robo-signing" (forging signatures on) mortgage foreclosure documents.[419] Because of the number of bank employees involved, because of the number of documents involved (tens of thousands), and because it involved five different businesses, it is difficult to imagine that top management had not signed off on this practice.

An ethics shortfall in American business is not new:

[1890s] But the democracy born of free land, strong in selfishness and individualism . . . [and with a] lack of a highly developed civic spirit . . . permitting lax business honor . . .[420]

—*Frederick Jackson Turner*

These comments about business ethics, CSR, do not apply to all businesses. Often, small or medium-sized American businesses are owned by individuals who feel a responsibility to their community (they have group identity). Such businesses may be managed with a high level of CSR.

Religion provides another exception to the comments that have been made regarding ethics. Some business managers and other individuals who accept our values of individualism, competition, and success may uphold high ethical standards because they believe that is consistent with their religious beliefs.

And some individuals and business managers have absorbed different values (culture) and they believe that ethical principles simply outweigh competition and success. But whatever the exceptions, they are not large enough to keep the United States from ranking near the bottom on the CSR index mentioned above.

Compared to American workers, Nordic workers are four times as likely to be union members (about 52 percent versus about 14 percent).[421] People don't park their culture outside when they walk through the door at work. Compared to their counterparts in the United States, Nordic management and labor are more likely to be cooperative.[422] Both sides work for improved working conditions and for improved efficiency. When management and unions cooperate it is similar to "flat management": the people affected by decisions are part of the decision-making process.

In contrast, with American individualism, and assuming that money equals success, an adversarial relationship between unions and management is natural. A dollar gained by one side is lost by the other.

Graduate students from the Carlson School of Management at the University of Minnesota who studied

Finnish businesses found: companies often benefit from a close relationship with government, innovation and employee input are actively encouraged, marketing is not as advanced as in the United States, and companies have longer-term strategies (less focused on quarterly reports). This is because of culture.[423]

> Only two and a half million tons of ore a year [in 1930 from a Swedish mine] may be taken out under present regulations. The young assistant manager, who had worked in American mines, said they could get several times that; had an almost American scorn for any plan to save something for his grandchildren.[424]
>
> —*Harry A. Franck*

A short-term business strategy may be a natural outcome of the free market, which rewards price efficiency at the expense of quality. Quality is more efficient long-term, but it requires a greater investment over a longer period.[425]

American investors' short-term perspective (including mutual funds competing for the fastest portfolio appreciation) may have encouraged CEO pay based on stock options and bonuses that are tied to stock prices. Presumably, CEOs' motivation is their pay (money equals status), and because of these options and bonuses, much of that pay is heavily influenced by quarterly reports.[426] Innovation and development, which might not yield a profit for years, could negatively impact an American CEO's pay. A shorter-term business strategy is natural.

[1920s] The American businessman is not content with merely making a living. He is interested in the immediate gain which he himself is able to extract in the process, and he discounts heavily any long-term motives.[427]

—*Thorstein Veblen*

For a Nordic CEO, money does not equal status, and there are other motivations besides pay. Culture, including practical thinking, encourages a longer-term business strategy.

Should we invest in a new casino, or should we invest in educating poor children? An individual or a company contemplating an investment should understand the "time value of money." Simply stated, because of interest, a dollar today is worth more than a dollar next year. An investor can assume a given interest rate and calculate whether it pays to invest a specific number of dollars today when a specific return is expected at some time in the future. This concept raises several questions:

(a) How do you estimate future interest rates? If historical rates are used, what time period is appropriate?

(b) What alternative investment opportunities exist—and are they equally safe?

(c) What is the potential cost of not investing? (Your car needs tires, or your business needs new equipment.)

(d) What level of inflation is anticipated? Likely, the Consumer Price Index understates actual inflation, but by how much? If the historical record is used, what time period should be used? Inflation negates interest because money becomes worth less, so an estimated interest rate of 8 percent and an estimated inflation rate of 4 percent leaves an estimated real interest rate of 4 percent; (with compound interest) $1.00 today is worth $2.00 in eighteen years.

(e) How do you accurately estimate the expected return in ten or twenty years?

For a group identity investor there are additional questions:

(f) Do alternative investments produce something of equal or greater value?

(g) How does this investment decision affect the environment, labor, industry, and the public?

There are two reasons for exploring these questions. First, in many or most cases, because there are so many unknowns, the time value of money is essentially subjective; one might easily imagine that it is a sophisticated rationalization to justify American investors' strong preference for short-term investing.[428] When compared with their American counterparts, if (as commonly acknowledged) Nordic buildings are constructed with a longer-term perspective, and if Nordic businesses have longer-term strategies, it is not because the time value of money is different on the east side of the Atlantic Ocean. More likely, it is because long-term is related to practical thinking.[429]

[In 1750, compared with Nordic homes] here [England] all the warmth goes freely up the chimney; windows, doors, roof, floor, etc., are not stopped or made tight, but the wind and cold get freely to play through them.[430]

—*Peter Kalm*

The second reason for examining these questions is to raise (but not resolve) the issue of whether all investments are equal. Relating to question (f) above: Does a typical investment (real estate or stocks), where the goal is short-term asset appreciation, have the same value as a long-term investment in a socially responsible industry that will employ people and produce a valuable product? Is it equally valuable for a bank to employ ten people trading derivatives (exotic financial wagering) as it is for the same bank to employ ten people searching for good small businesses to loan to?[431]

In the development of the United States the typical businessman was a small dealer in real estate . . . the essence of this business is to get something for nothing . . .[432]

—*Thorstein Veblen*

Relating to question (g) above: investing in a casino might bring almost certain profits and bring them quickly; investing additional dollars educating poor children might not return anything for years, and when it did, the return would be difficult to measure. But a recent study by Art Rolnick and Rob Grunewald of the Federal Reserve Bank of Minneapolis found that every $1 invested in the early childhood education of poor children returned $8 (mostly to the benefit of the general public).[433]

Both Americans and Nordic people are generous and want to help people in other countries; for example, the top six positions on the Commitment to Development Index 2011 are held by the United States, four Nordic countries and the Netherlands (see Chapter Eleven). Beyond that, American and Nordic worldviews are different.

It is common for Americans to assume that we lead the world in progress, that our military is the most powerful, and that other countries should attempt to emulate us (adopt our American ideology). Often, Americans have little interest in the rest of the world: Polish-American political scientist and statesman Zbigniew Brzezinski has used the word *abysmal* to sum up Americans' knowledge of other countries.[434]

America has benefited from friendly and smaller neighbors; large oceans to the east and west, Mexico to the south, and Canada to the north. We have long been the biggest fish in our part of the pond while the Nordic countries have been, and are, small fish swimming among much larger fish. Denmark, Norway, and Finland were each invaded in the mid-twentieth century, and Finland lost significant territory at that time. Denmark was invaded in the mid-nineteenth century and, as a result, lost significant territory. Sweden was invaded in the early nineteenth century and lost Finland at that time.

As in their own governments, Nordic countries are calm and respectful toward their neighbors. They do not react to their neighbors based on concepts of good and evil;[435] instead Nordic countries are practical—what works best long-term? Sometimes, for a small fish "what works best" may be a shade of gray (not ideal).[436]

Nordic people are interested in and knowledgeable about other countries. As a tourist in 2002, this writer picked up a daily paper in Stockholm that contained a several-page story about what it is like to be a woman in Afghanistan. A Swedish reporter had gone there, lived with families (a week or more at a time), and attempted to learn about the life of Afghani women. Two weeks later, a daily paper in Oslo carried a lengthy article about Palestinians attempting to drive to Palestinian hospitals; about four people a month were dying while they waited to get through Israeli checkpoints in Palestinian territory. If a daily American newspaper printed an in-depth article such as these, would most subscribers read it?[437]

> Rationalism permeates the content of [Swedish] radio and television programs and the editorial and opinion pages of large newspapers.[438]
>
> —*Åke Daun*

When asked if they followed politics in the news (radio, television, newspapers), yes responses were: Sweden 72 percent, Denmark 64 percent, Iceland 45 percent, Finland 39 percent, and United States 34 percent (no figures were listed for Norway).[439] The low response from the United States is confirmed by voter turnout rates (mentioned elsewhere) in congressional elections from 1960 to 1995.[440] A lack of interest in other countries (and our own politics) might reflect ideologies: if one is free from thinking, there is no need to be interested in or read about other countries.

A typical American student's worldview (or the absence of one) is significant; reportedly, ignorance of other countries and their history, inexperience in cross-cultural communication, and a shortfall in foreign language skills threatens our economy and our national security.[441]

Chapter Twelve mentioned that Nordic landowners accept public (government) forest management. Up until about 1900, Nordic forests were not managed and were heavily utilized for heating fuel, lumber for buildings, charcoal for iron smelting, pulp for paper, and other uses. About a hundred years ago, forest management legislation was passed in Denmark, Finland, Norway, and Sweden.

The effect of the new legislation was to manage forests for long-term sustainability by regulating replanting after harvest, what species were planted, when trees were to be harvested, etc. In the last half century, the goal of forest management has broadened to include protection of endangered species' habitat, biodiversity, ecology, and carbon management.[442]

Nordic forest management is scientific and highly practical. For example, harvesting is timed with available industrial capacity and with the commercial demand for specific products. Even periodic wind storms are factored into forest management.[443] Every five to ten years there is a windstorm that damages large areas of forest. Past experience and scientific studies, together with professional workers and equipment from other countries, are all utilized to harvest storm-damaged trees before the wood can degrade. Within a short time after a storm, forest management officials are able to firmly estimate the loss (in cubic meters) and to pinpoint the locations where the harvest will take place.

Statistically comparing American and Nordic forest production would be tedious. Instead, for the sake of simplicity, Minnesota will be compared to Sweden. Sweden has 71 million acres of forests: 50 percent is owned by private individuals, 25 percent is owned by private companies, and 25 percent is publicly owned. A tiny fraction of the forests, 0.3 percent, is strictly protected with no human intervention allowed.

In the mid-1800s when Minnesota became a state, forests covered half of it, and today the wood products industry is Minnesota's fourth largest industry. About 47 percent of Minnesota's forests are privately owned and the balance is publicly owned (federal, state, counties, municipalities). Annual forest production has been declining because of the economy; it totaled about 2.8 million cords in 2008.[444]

On public lands, forest management is fragmented by which unit of government owns the land, and it is further fragmented by goals or objectives. No state or federal laws mandate forest management for private landowners in Minnesota.[445] There are no laws in effect for dealing with the significant problem of invasive species such as buckthorn.

A decade or more ago, the Minnesota Department of Natural Resources (DNR) had forty foresters (or full-time equivalents) available to advise private landowners on tree planting, trail systems, culverts, invasive species, and establishment of stewardship plans (typically a ten-year management plan). For a small fee, foresters also helped arrange timber sales. Today, with less funding, the number of foresters is ten or twelve and, generally, stewardship plans are no longer available.[446]

In the past there have been state and federal grant funds available to private landowners for tree planting (such as in the 1950s and 1960s). Now, state grant funds are gone, and federal grant funds have diminished.

Sweden's annual harvest is about 95 million cubic meters of wood on 71 million acres, while Minnesota's annual harvest (average during the last decade) is about 3.5 million cords of wood on 15.6 million acres. If there are 2.3 cubic meters of wood in a cord, then Minnesota produces .516 cubic meters of wood per year per acre, and Sweden produces 1.338 cubic meters of wood per year per acre. But Sweden is located about 15 degrees of latitude (roughly a thousand miles) farther north; probably trees grow significantly more slowly there. If that is true, the actual difference attributable to scientific forest management is greater than the ratio of 1.338 (Sweden) to .516 (Minnesota).

Forest management is long-term. The process from the time a tree is planted until it has reached a desirable harvest size takes many decades, in some cases more than a century. With *individualism*, planting trees, protecting them from fire, controlling competing vegetation, and thinning are actual expenses for which landowners may never see any actual return (in their lifetime). American landowners who practice careful forest management are altruistic; rather than for their own benefit, they are doing something for future generations.

With *group identity*, long-term forest management is practical rather than altruistic. The group (society) isn't going anywhere, and when trees are harvested, individual landowners benefit from a larger harvest and because the harvest is coordinated with both available industrial capacity and demand.

And, would harvesting and processing businesses be more likely to invest in better equipment if they could depend on an assured supply of a specific type and grade of raw material? Better harvesting and processing equipment could yield a higher return, some of which might find its way back to the landowner.

> He [the American] has been an opportunist rather than a dealer in general ideas. Destiny set him in a current which bore him swiftly along through such a wealth of opportunity that reflection and well-considered planning seemed wasted time.[447]
>
> —*Frederick Jackson Turner*

Rather than continuing with more examples, readers may wish to review the chart in Chapter Eleven that shows how America ranks on the various progress indexes. Compared with all of the nations of the world we rank near the top in most measures of progress. But the Nordic countries along with Australia, Canada, Germany, Netherlands, New Zealand, and Switzerland are stiffer competition; we don't necessarily rank at the top compared with them.[448] If that was the whole story we would be finished, but it is not. We have compared America with its abundant resources to Nordic countries that (excepting Norway's oil)[449] have only limited resources. What would happen if conditions changed?

America, "from sea to shining sea," had belonged to Indians, but they were shunted aside. The early colonists and later immigrants inherited a land rich in resources: fish and game, timber, fresh water, a favorable climate, vast quantities of productive farmland, grasslands, waterways, coal, iron, copper, gold, silver, oil, natural gas—even friendly neighbors. Not just resources, but abundant resources, and in some cases ideally located. Huge deposits of high-grade iron ore were separated by navigable water from large deposits of coal. America was blessed.

> Not the constitution, but free land and an abundance of natural resources open to a fit people, made the democratic society in America.[450]

> —*Frederick Jackson Turner*

As late as World War II, our needs for these resources, including war use, could be satisfied by our own supply. Because of providing war material, we ended World War II with most of the world's supply of gold along with considerable foreign investments (debts owed to us). The United States was the world's largest creditor; we had powerful industries and a talented work force; we could supply all of our own resources: America was rich.

American ideology has always operated in a resource-rich environment, but that has begun to change in the last half century. Today, the old-growth forests are almost gone, the high-grade iron ore deposits are gone, and we import about one third of the oil we consume every day. Our manufacturing sector has diminished and we import huge quantities of autos, electronics, clothes, and other items; so much so that our imports—mostly for personal consumption—exceed our exports by up to $2 billion every day. We are borrowing from foreigners to maintain our standard of living. Today we are the world's biggest debtor.

What would happen if we could not borrow from foreigners and had to live within our means? What would happen if we were cut off from foreign oil? What would happen if Americans decided that it was imperative to significantly reduce carbon emissions? What if our economy was damaged by a breakdown in trust (in government, business, religion, or because of income inequality)? What would happen if globalization led to a shrinking U.S. economy (less resource consumption)? Each of these possibilities sounds unlikely, but it is difficult to imagine significant change until after it happens.

With abundant resources, American ideology produces a virtual cornucopia of consumer goods and a high standard of living for many people. Our culture is designed for abundant resources, and we equate money with status, but to show that one has money—to establish one's status—it is necessary to buy something.[451] Actually it's a little more complicated: it helps to buy conspicuously bigger, better or more than one needs. A Norwegian American educator and author thought that Americans had inherited this value, "conspicuous waste," from the English.

> [T]he conspicuously wasteful consumption of the [English] gentleman must not incidentally or by leakage conduce in any degree to the physical well-being . . . of anyone else.[452]
>
> —*Thorstein Veblen*

Maybe the success attributed to our ideology is dependent upon abundant resources. What would happen in the (difficult to imagine) event that American ideology was paired with more limited resources? For example, what if our oil consumption was reduced from about twenty-two barrels per capita per year to the average level of Canada, Japan, France, Germany, Italy, and the United Kingdom, about thirteen barrels per capita per year? We are competitive with these countries in measures of progress now, but would we be competitive if we consumed only the same level of resources as they do?

Perhaps the importance of abundant resources to American ideology is reflected in social mobility statistics. A 2005 study by Jason Long and Joseph Ferrie (National Bureau of Economic Research) found that in the 1800s social mobility—equal opportunity—was three times higher in America (with free land and an expanding frontier) than it was in the UK. By 1950 social mobility was similar in both countries, and today social mobility is higher in the UK than in the United States.[453]

[On the American frontier] These free lands promoted individualism, economic equality, freedom to rise [social mobility], democracy.[454]

—*Frederick Jackson Turner*

Apparently, Americans experienced group identity during World War II. After Pearl Harbor, in the face of an immediate foreign threat, we united, sacrificed for the common good, and worked together to defeat the enemy. An excess profits tax on business, a steeply progressive income tax, rationing that applied to everyone, and military conscription that was perceived to be fair allowed Americans to feel that everyone was involved. It was a group effort—we achieved a group identity.[455]

This group identity included the same principles (mutual responsibilities) as was earlier attributed to Nordic people, including cooperation. (Probably, the generation that came of age during this period never completely abandoned those principles.) Social pressure played a part; for example, a man who attempted to avoid the draft, or someone who engaged in black market activities, was looked down on. Their social status fell, and others may have been reluctant to socialize with them.

What if the United States faced a serious threat, but instead of a foreign enemy, the threat was actually a number of issues, which—together—amounted to a serious long-term threat? Issues that might threaten our nation include pollution, climate change, income inequality (and the resulting loss of trust),[456] failure to conserve resources, global competition, the balance of payments deficit, and education.

We were leaders in education, but that day is gone; the United States is—today—being outcompeted in education. That is the subject of a 2012 report, *U.S. Education Reform and National Security* (Joel I. Klein, Condoleezza Rice, chairs). In this report, the majority recommends (among other things) more competition and more testing.

America's K–12 schools had been predominantly public, but in response to real problems that surfaced in recent decades—ignoring culture, which contributed to those problems—politicians have urged more choice (competition) and more testing.[457] The intent is to reshape K–12 education into a corporate mold, an approximation of the free market.[458]

Our free market produces short-term cost efficiency; to the extent that K–12 education can be subjected to the free market, the cost of education would fall. However, the free market does not encourage quality, and choice combined with testing has not produced quality.[459] Our free-market ideology has produced an unequal society, and we should expect the same result in education.[460]

This report mentions culture (socioeconomic conditions, growing inequality, low teacher status, declining social mobility) but then ignores those factors in the majority's recommendations. For example, the report points out that teachers have relatively low prestige (status), making it more difficult to attract and keep the most talented individuals.[461] But, money equals success in American culture; to the extent that other occupations enjoy higher pay, they would also have higher prestige. More competition and more testing won't change that.

Nordic education reflects Nordic culture, and money is not the sole (or even the principal) measure of success.[462] In Finland, teachers have higher status than doctors and other professionals, education is not centrally controlled, teachers play a key role in innovation, and there is collaboration between education and industry.[463] A holistic approach (including almost no poverty), a strong group identity ("social cohesion"), and equality are fundamental to Finnish education.[464] Stressing methods that are the opposite of U.S. methods, Finnish education is arguably the best in the world.[465]

The *U.S. Education Reform and National Security* report concludes that—because of students' ignorance of foreign countries, because of students' lack of foreign language skills, because of a shortfall in engineering graduates, and because of inequality in education—American K–12 education is a threat to our economy and to our national security.

Two other issues, global competition and pollution, will be briefly mentioned. Generally, pollution cannot be successfully addressed without violating free-market ideology. People, acting through their elected representatives, may force change, and some companies exhibit group identity (principles); otherwise many companies have the money and the marketing sophistication to forestall pollution abatement indefinitely. International pollution is common. Industries in the northern United States may cause acid rain in Canada. American companies, to increase profits, may ship toxic waste to third world countries. Americans breathe air that contains pollutants from Asia. Clearly, each individual (or company) following selfish motives cannot solve pollution.

Increasingly, American companies are directly competing with foreign companies. As was mentioned earlier, because American health care is so expensive, it has an important role in this competition. Typically, a foreign company pays nothing for health care (its employees either have state health care or they have no health care), while an American employer might pay $10,000 or more per year, per employee. On top of that, wage rates in the United States might be higher because of union contracts while wage rates in a foreign country might be artificially low because of a manipulated currency; companies (or industries) sometimes receive government subsidies; taxes may be equivalent to a tariff; pollution requirements vary; paperwork varies. Individual companies have little control over the global marketplace, but government leadership could make it easier for American companies to compete. If that happened it would produce more American jobs, but it would violate our free-market ideology.

Pollution, climate change, income inequality, conservation of resources, global competition, the balance of payments deficit, and education share a common thread with a foreign enemy—although each individual must do his or her part, these issues cannot be successfully addressed by individuals simply pursuing their self-interest in competition with one another. These issues require government leadership, but that has no chance of success unless there is the same type of group identity that Americans were able to achieve during World War II. Without group identity (and social pressure) that impacts everyone, including business leaders and government employees, government efforts to address these issues would surely fail.

What if the United States was confronted by multiple issues, none of which (by itself) constituted an immediate serious threat, and which could not be addressed by everyone pursuing his or her own selfish motives? Without an immediate foreign threat, would or could Americans embrace group identity?

14

Summary

In Chapter One, it was claimed that an understanding of Nordic culture has the potential to improve human lives. That potential might be realized through knowledge and dialogue. Knowledge—an understanding of both Nordic culture and our own—could enrich discussions of important issues in the United States. To that end, the Nordic values described earlier will be briefly reviewed and contrasted with relevant American values.

It is natural for women to be independent.

In the Nordic countries an ancient tradition of independent women has evolved into an actively sought goal of gender equality. Here gender equality is consistent with equal treatment for everyone, a classless society. An equal role for women encourages a society to be more cooperative, more empathetic, and more adverse to conflict; it also encourages it to attempt to resolve issues through dialogue.[466] And, women find it easier to accept change.

[1930] The Finns are quick to adopt modern methods of eliminating unnecessary manual labor. There is no prejudice against any proper means of improving the state of the nation, nor any disposition to abide by traditions when reason points to the wisdom of their abandonment.[467]

—Harry A. Franck

Over the last century in the United States, women's status has changed significantly. In the early years of the twentieth century married women were supposed to be dependent; for example, female school teachers had to give up their career if they married. In 1950, the most accepted careers for women were teacher, secretary, and nurse. Today, for most Americans, it is natural for married women to work outside of the home. Today, women are as likely, or even more likely, to graduate from college, and women's participation in most professions is high or increasing.

But, as in other areas, our value is equal opportunity, not equality. We are becoming a less equal society, and, probably, many Americans do not really believe in gender equality. We lag behind the Nordic countries on this value, which is interconnected with other attitudes and values.

It is natural for children to be responsible for themselves—independent—at an early age.

This value is visible in many sources that deal with Scandinavian immigrants. It helps promote education and equality as well as encouraging mutual responsibilities. It appears self-evident that independent young adults would be more inclined to take chances, more inclined to innovate, more inclined to move to a new location.[468] It is safe to say that the old-time patriarchal extended families (where children never became independent) were the most averse to change, and the Nordic-style family is at the opposite extreme.

Americans have not had the same emphasis on children becoming independent at an early age. Reportedly, because of a difficult economy, almost one-third of today's college graduates will move back into their parent's home after graduation.[469] Difficult economy or not, these American children are not yet independent.[470]

This value difference is reflected in the observation, mentioned earlier, that Nordic students want to be independent while American students want to be well liked.[471] This difference encourages American students to be less practical in their choices (college, career, etc.).[472]

Children must be educated.

Because Nordic people were not completely settled, because they exploited diverse resources, and because children became independent early, children had to be taught a variety of skills including reading and arithmetic. Authority belonged to the people, and children became adults quickly—they had to be educated. Children were raised knowing that they would have to depend on themselves: they needed to learn. Over time, these old-time values morphed into making education, including college, available to all.

Not all Americans were completely settled, but many of them pursued just one occupation; sons could learn from their fathers, and daughters could learn from their mothers. At the same time authority, as evidenced by voting, frequently came from above, and top-down authority inhibits education. Basic education including reading and arithmetic was important but some Americans did without. Those circumstances morphed into making education compulsory, often to age sixteen, while college was available to those who were motivated and could arrange financing. One exception occurred after World War II when the GI Bill made college available to millions of veterans, and as a result the United States led the world in college graduates—then.[473]

Everyone, regardless of wealth or status, is equal.

Through taxation, legislation, and social pressure, Nordic societies are among the most equal in the world. There are differences in wealth and status but everyone is supposed to be treated equally. This value is handed down unconsciously, and it is taught in schools where children are not graded the first six years, apparently to insure that all are treated equally. Equality is the foundation for interpersonal trust and for group identity.

American culture includes equal opportunity: everyone is supposed to have a chance to improve his or her position in society. The civil rights movement resulted in increased equality for Blacks and other minorities. Laws against various types of discrimination, and laws mandating quotas for college admissions or hiring on government contracts are, or were, steps toward equality for minorities. Marriage rights for gays and anti-bullying efforts in schools are incremental steps toward equality.

On the other hand, if any American ideology encourages one to feel that one is part of an exclusive group, or if an ideology encourages one to feel superior to others, that is negative for equality. And our increasing income inequality over the last fifty years makes us less and less equal—a much richer upper class is effectively an aristocracy. According to a recent book, *The Spirit Level*, by Wikinson and Pickett, our high level of income inequality influences a number of social problems.

As equal members of a group, all share mutual responsibilities.

Nordic group identity with mutual responsibilities was encouraged by children becoming independent at an early age.[474] Old-time rural life required both cooperation and consensus; it wouldn't take long to learn to be respectful and see things from others' point of view if you absolutely needed their cooperation. And, mutual respect must have been healthy for ancient Nordic people who attended their legislative/judicial *ting* armed. Here again consensus was often necessary.

Nordic group identity with mutual responsibilities is "natural." For most of human history, people have depended on mutual responsibilities for their very existence. Group identity with mutual responsibilities always existed at the family or community level: it is human nature. And throughout our human history, equal societies are the rule, not the exception.[475]

American individualism with its emphasis on competition, is the opposite of Nordic group identity with its emphasis on cooperation. With group identity, cooperation, respect, truthfulness, fairness, and empathy are expected and also reinforced by social pressure. With competitive individualism, ethical principles are often altruistic—adhering to principles can lead to lost revenue, loss of competitive advantage, or loss of a job. For example, if an employee complained to his or her superior that the company was being unethical to customers, it would likely have a negative impact on that employee's career.

On both sides of the Atlantic Ocean social pressure plays an important role in this value. Nordic people feel pressure to not stand out from the group; any self-important behavior will not go unnoticed. Social pressure encourages Americans to compete, to be ambitious, to "keep up with the Joneses."

A good story is realistic and contains a message.

Elsewhere in Europe, written stories began with upper-class men (only they were literate) writing idealized stories that promoted theology or that entertained readers. Nordic writers were ordinary people who continued an oral tradition of realistic stories that contained a message. Writing was a tool that could be used to teach a value.

The Icelandic sagas (recorded A.D.1100–1350) were unique.[476] They taught history and they taught culture, expectations of what behavior was acceptable and what was not. The popular book, *The Girl with the Dragon Tattoo*, was intended by its author, Stieg Larsson, to highlight a social issue: violence against women. Larsson's title for his book, translated from Swedish, is *The Man Who Hated Women*.

In 1748 Finnish naturalist Peter Kalm wrote of the American colonies, "it was everybody's sole care and employment to scrape a fortune together, and where the sciences were held in universal contempt."[477] Attending college in Ann Arbor, Michigan, in 1931, a young Swede, Raoul Wallenberg, was disparaging in his comments about American newspapers.[478] Probably we do not feel any great need for practical thinking, so there is nothing wrong with news reports that are intended to entertain and amuse.

All things considered, what works best?

In the Nordic region, practical thinking, or time consciousness or being organized, was encouraged by the environment: a shortage of good cropland, a very short growing season, long winters, a mosaic of land and water, powerful neighbors, lifestyle, and more. For example, crops needed to be planted and harvested on time. The growing season was so short, even if everything was done on time, crops might not mature. Insufficient cropland encouraged finding of other resources. Livestock needed to be cared for every day. Waterways encouraged boat building and trade. People were rewarded for practical thinking, and the punishment for not engaging in it would likely be hunger or worse.[479]

> The people knew how to face the long, severe winters, and there were not many who froze to death.
>
> —*Eric Norelius*

Equality played a role in practical thinking. In the past, elsewhere in Europe, decisions were made by men who were removed from the daily struggle for existence. They could make whimsical decisions without it taking the bread off of their table. Not so in the Nordic region: here ordinary people made the decisions that affected their own lives— flat management.

America's founding fathers embraced Enlightenment ideals and rejected visible class distinctions such as titles, but—based on voting—the reality continued to be top-down authority. To this day, Americans have not completely rejected top-down authority, and that inhibits practical thinking. And we continue to embrace ideals or ideologies that also inhibit practical thinking.

But environment might be the most important factor: America had abundant resources, especially free land. America's bounty provided opportunities that did not require long-term planning and careful calculations. Practical thinking was not necessary.

All have a voice; laws and institutions are necessary; justice rules.

It would be easy to imagine that in a warrior society (ancient Nordic people) this value would reduce conflict, and no doubt that is true. Another explanation (no warrior society needed) is Todd's concept that authority mirrors family structure.[480] People who are subject to one authority (family patriarch, religious leader, etc.) are more likely to accept top-down political authority. On the other hand, independent individuals expect to participate in, have a voice in, their own government. Clearly, to the extent that a patriarch, prince, or religious leader holds authority, to that same extent laws and institutions merely facilitate that person's rule. Laws, institutions, and justice are only effective to the extent that authority belongs to people as a group.

The United States was founded on the ideal that authority belongs to the people: "We the People of the United States . . . do ordain and establish this CONSTITUTION," and the Constitution embodies the concept of equal justice. According to President John Adams, our ideal is:

A government of laws and not of men.

But, as has been mentioned repeatedly, this ideal was not and is not reality. Four decades after the Constitution became law, less than 5 percent of the population voted. Over the last century voting privileges have been greatly enlarged, yet in many elections today less than half of the eligible voters actually cast a ballot.

American acceptance of top-down authority was evident in Stanley Milgram's experiments in the 1960s; that same acceptance had astonished a young Swede, Raoul Wallenberg, three decades earlier. Today, apparently, we are so accustomed to top-down authority that there is little protest when special privileges are awarded to wealthy individuals and large corporations. Possible examples of such special privileges include: tax cuts for wealthy individuals in the face of widening inequality between rich and poor; price guarantees for pharmaceutical companies in Medicare Part D; tax breaks for long-established oil companies; no indictments of executives in the housing crisis that forced thousands from their homes, including "robo-signing"; and protection of the status of health insurers in the 2010 health care reform legislation. To whatever extent this legislation favors wealthy individuals and large corporations at the expense of ordinary voters, to that extent authority is top-down.

> From each according to ability, to each according to need.[481]

> *—Sverige & Svenskarna*

From an American perspective, there are negative side affects to the Nordic culture described in these pages. As mentioned earlier, equality implies social leveling, social pressure. At its worst, this takes the form of *Janteloven* (the law of Jante), a fictitious harangue against the social pressure to not stand out from the group. *Janteloven* represents a stereotype from the first half of the twentieth century, but even with a more moderate interpretation, this type of social pressure would be alien to Americans.

Social leveling is a significant factor in progress indexes that measure wealth or prosperity because these indexes use a formula (a "mean") rather than an average. These indexes are adjusted so that the wealth of a few does not hide the poverty of many. And, Nordic social welfare programs play a significant role in indexes related to health and education. These programs are paid for with taxes, usually including a high national sales tax.

Some present-day immigrants and some descendants of earlier immigrants understand that the homeland culture was unique and valuable. Many descendants appreciate the courage and determination with which the immigrants overcame the challenges they faced. Beyond that there is limited appreciation that Scandinavian immigrants were essentially different from other immigrants, and different from earlier Americans, "Yankees."

Scandinavian immigrants were different because of culture, and they were different in a good way. They took for granted an independent role for women; they assumed children would be on their own at an early age; they placed a high value on education; they were honest and truthful; they were experienced cooperators; they felt mutual sympathy and mutual responsibility; they believed in law and justice; they were literate; they were accustomed to democracy; they were practical. They assumed that one must travel to find work or to exploit resources. In the New World this could mean working in a lumber camp for the winter, or moving from their first home in America to California or Cuba or Saskatchewan or Alaska.

There are ample reasons for their descendants to be proud of the immigrants, but the real significance of Nordic culture is not pride (family, ethnic, or national). Instead, the real significance of Nordic culture, the reason it is worth exploring, is because it works.

Denmark, Finland, Iceland, Norway, and Sweden have generally insufficient natural resources; they have an uncomfortable climate, an inconvenient geography, sometimes unfriendly neighbors, and they speak languages that are unintelligible to the rest of the world. And yet, Nordic culture has produced prosperity, quality education and health care for all, near gender equality, numerous advances in technology, and transparent and democratic government—all of the things that most people associate with progress. And Nordic progress is not just ordinary progress: it is world-class progress.

A basic understanding of Nordic culture as well as some understanding of our own culture, why we do things the way we do, could enrich discussions on many current issues. It could benefit Americans.

Appendix: About the Cover

As I gave some weight to population, one person was chosen from Iceland, three from Sweden, and two each from Denmark, Finland, and Norway. These individuals are, or were, well-known, otherwise there were no specific guidelines for this selection. Sources for the following brief sketches include publications, books, and Wikipedia and other Internet sites, as well as other sources.

Ingrid Bergman (1915–1982)

Ingrid Bergman was one of a number of Swedish actresses including Greta Garbo, Anita Ekberg, and Ann-Margret who became stars in American movies. Bergman was born in Stockholm to an artist/photographer father and a German immigrant mother. Both her parents died young, and Bergman lived for a time with two of her aunts before she was old enough to be independent.

As a child she knew she wanted to act, and, after winning an acting competition at age 17, Bergman was awarded a scholarship to the Royal Dramatic Theatre School. However, she did not complete the standard three-year-course; instead she began acting and had her first role in a film, *Munkbrogreven*, at age nineteen. Bergman quickly became a leading actress in Swedish films.

Although unable to speak English, the twenty-four-year-old Bergman came to Hollywood and within a few years had lead roles in half a dozen American movies including *Casablanca* (1942) co-starring Humphrey Bogart. This was not Bergman's favorite film, but it has been credited with being one of the best movies of all-time and is still shown on TV.

Bergman did not like makeup artists, as she did not want anyone to change her appearance, and she was strong willed enough to have her way. Bergman did not change either her face or her name to suit Hollywood, but she became a well-known and popular celebrity.

In 1950, while starring in an Italian film, Bergman had an affair with its director, Roberto Rossellini. Both were already married, and Bergman had a twelve-year-old daughter by her first husband. This was too much for some Americans who, partly because of the roles she had played (she was a nun in *The Bells of St. Mary's*) thought of her as almost a saint. Because of this affair, a few American theaters refused to show her films, and she was shunned by a TV show.

During her career Bergman did movies in five different languages and won three Academy Awards. She was a "natural," so talented that movie-goers had difficulty separating Bergman the actor from the roles she played.

Niels Bohr (1885–1962)

Niels Bohr's mother came from a family of prominent Danish educators; his father, who inspired Niels to study physics, was a professor of physiology in Copenhagen. Bohr received his master's degree in physics in 1909, his doctor's degree in1911, and continued his studies at Cambridge and Manchester, England.

In 1920 Bohr was appointed head of the Institute for Theoretical Physics (established for him) at Copenhagen University. In recognition of his work, Bohr was awarded the 1922 Nobel Prize in Physics.

> Everything we call real is made of things that cannot be regarded as real.
>
> —*Niels Bohr*

Niels Bohr was the father of quantum physics. He along with a few other scientists developed theories and formulas that explain how matter and energy behave at the subatomic level. According to this writer's son, Jim B. Hove, quantum physics is impossible to visualize—imagine creating a mental image of a probability wave, but the "Copenhagen School" says that we can forget about visualizing and just use the theories and formulas.

Bohr's research and ideas have been published in English including three books: *The Theory of Spectra and Atomic Consitution* (1922), *Atomic Theory and the Description of Nature* (1934), and *Atomic Views and Human Knowledge* (1958).

During World War II, Bohr fled to Sweden to escape the Nazis and ended up in the United States where he was associated with the Atomic Energy Project. He devoted his efforts toward the peaceful uses of atomic energy and solving the political issues raised by atomic physics. In an open letter to the United Nations in 1950, Bohr advocated international openness, communication, and cooperation to avoid the potential consequences of nuclear armaments.

Bohr's interpretation of quantum physics led him into a vigorous debate with Albert Einstein. Einstein believed that Bohr's interpretation could not be complete because, if it were, the physics principle of "locality" would be violated. While they were alive it was impossible to resolve this debate, but a later physicist, John Stewart Bell, was able to establish that both men were correct: Bohr's interpretation was correct, and it was true that the "locality" principle was violated.

N.F.S. Grundtvig (1783–1872)

N.F.S. Grundtvig was a multitalented theologian and pastor who lived for almost ninety years. Rather than attempt even a brief summary of his life and work, this sketch will be limited to a few paragraphs about religion and education; these are based primarily on the writing of Joy Ibsen who is, however, not responsible for any errors.[482]

> We work at becoming human beings. Christianity is a gift.
>
> —*Axel Kildegaard*

Many American descendants of Danish immigrants are familiar with Grundtvig's "Human first then Christian" teaching, which referred to separation rather than priority. As humans we should be happy, enjoy our humanity, appreciate nature's beauty, and find joy in everyday life; as humans we should be realistic and work to resolve issues such as equality, environment, and education; and as humans we should respect and tolerate other religions. But, being "Human first" does not reduce the importance of Christianity.

Grundtvig believed that the spoken word and congregations preceded the Bible. The Bible had not created the church, but rather the church had created the Bible. He emphasized the Apostles' Creed because it was straightforward and not as easy to "twist" as the Bible, which was subject to interpretation. Grundtvig taught that Christ is alive, in the congregation, in baptism, and in communion.

During his era, ordinary people attended elementary schools for perhaps six years, and above that, education was restricted to the upper class. Grundtvig was highly critical of this education system because it was elitist; it was top-down with little dialog between professor and students; and it emphasized memorizing, testing, and book learning.

Grundtvig made an enduring contribution to education when he created the Folk School movement aimed at adult ordinary people who were not eligible for any further formal education. Students at these schools came together when farm work was less demanding to learn from teachers and from each other. Dialog between students as well as between students and teachers was fundamental; teachers were not "above" the students. The goal was lifelong practical and spiritual learning.

Eventually hundreds of Folk Schools were established throughout the Nordic countries, and there are to this day hundreds of these schools providing learning opportunities for adult students. Danish immigrants brought this concept to the New World, and a few Folk Schools were established in the United States.

Tarja Halonen

Born in 1943 in a working class neighborhood of Helsinki, Tarja Halonen grew up with an appreciation of working class values. She graduated from the University of Helsinki in 1968 with a master of laws degree. She first worked for a credit firm, then as an officer of the National Union of University Students. This position influenced her to accept a position in 1970 as an attorney for the Finnish Trade Unions organization.

In 1974, Halonen was appointed parliamentary secretary to the prime minister (she was officially in politics). In 1976 she was elected to the Helsinki City Council, and in 1979 to the Finnish parliament. She was Chairman of the Social Committee from 1984 to 1987, and Minister of Social Affairs and Health starting in 1987, and also served for a time as Minister of Justice and Minister of Foreign Affairs.

In 1999 Halonen announced her intention to run for president, but she was not a typical candidate. Her political views were significantly to the left of center, she was in a long-term relationship (unmarried), she had a daughter from a previous relationship, and she had left the Finnish Lutheran Church because it refused to ordain women.

In the election, none of the candidates received a majority so a runoff was held, which Halonen won. On March 1st of 2000 Halonen became the first female President of Finland, and she held that post until 2012 when she was barred by law from seeking a third five-year term. Her elections were close, but public opinion polls showed that voters were favorably impressed with Halonen.

True to her upbringing, Halonen identified with the values of working people. She promoted gender equality issues, both in Finland and worldwide. She was active in human rights, and once served as chairman of SETA, a LGBT organization in Finland. She promoted good relations with Russia, was opposed to Finnish membership in NATO, and encouraged Finnish membership in the European Union. She speaks Finnish, Swedish, English, and she has studied Estonian. Halonen has received numerous international honors, and this writer was in the audience when Halonen received an honorary degree from the University of Minnesota Duluth in 2008.

Fridtjof Nansen (1861-1930)

Born in Christiania (Oslo), Norway, as a young man Fridtjof Nansen was a champion skier and skater. He was educated at the Royal Frederick University where his doctorial theses contributed to present-day theories of neurology. After 1896, his research area became oceanography.

In 1888 Nansen organized and led a small expedition that crossed Greenland on skis—the first ever to accomplish that. After returning home, Nansen began planning a larger expedition that included the possibility of reaching the North Pole. His preparations for this expedition were painstakingly thorough.

For this expedition, Nansen designed and built a small ship, the *Fram*, which could withstand the intense pressure exerted by Arctic ice. The *Fram* worked: it served Nansen well, and later it was used by Amundsen on both his successful transit of the Northwest Passage and on his successful Antarctic Expedition. Today the *Fram* is housed in a museum in Oslo.

Nansen's expedition (1893–1896) did not reach the North Pole but it proved that Arctic ice moves in a predictable pattern, something that was then a new theory. Nansen recorded many scientific measurements and observations, and thus provided the first reliable information about the Arctic.

During this expedition, Nansen spent one winter in a make-shift shelter; he described that experience as "boring." Reading Nansen's account of his polar expedition one is struck by the absence of heroic rhetoric; the scurvy and life-threatening danger that characterizes stories of American and English expeditions of this period is missing in Nansen's story. After three years in the Arctic, Nansen and his crew returned to Norway in good health.

Nansen was a well-rounded individual; in addition to being an explorer, scientist, and author (*Farthest North, In Northern Mists, Blant sel og bjørn*), he was also a humanitarian. In 1921 the League of Nations, predecessor of the United Nations, appointed him High Commissioner for Refugees. Nansen, an agnostic/atheist, spent the remainder of his life attempting to aid and resettle hundreds of thousands of World War I refugees. To that end, he developed the "Nansen Passport," which allowed refugees to travel in many countries where they could work and apply for permanent status. For his humanitarian service, Nansen was awarded the 1922 Nobel Peace Prize.

Alfred Nobel (1833–1896)

Born in Stockholm, Sweden, Alfred Nobel's father was an engineer and inventor while his mother at one time ran a grocery business to help support the family.

Before his twentieth birthday, Nobel was fluent in Russian, English, French, Swedish, and German. He traveled in many countries, but was somewhat introverted; his main interests were English literature, poetry, physics, and chemistry.

Following in his father's footsteps, Nobel began experimenting with explosives, especially nitroglycerine, a highly unstable liquid that had recently been invented by an Italian chemist. His experiments created several accidental explosions including one in 1864 that killed his brother and several workers. Nobel was undeterred: he continued experimenting and eventually mixed nitroglycerine with a substance that produced a paste that was stable, that didn't accidentally explode, and that could be molded into tubes. Nobel patented this product, which he called dynamite and, to detonate it, he invented a blasting cap that could be set off by lighting a fuse. Dynamite and blasting caps dramatically reduced the cost of digging canals and tunnels as well as building roads.

Nobel was a skilled entrepreneur and used his inventions, dynamite and others, to establish businesses that are visible today in names such as AB Bofors (Sweden), Imperial Chemical Industries (ICI in the UK), Dyno Industries (Norway), and Societe Centrale de Dynamite, (France). Nobel never lost interest in chemistry and physics, and he eventually held some 350 patents.

And he never lost interest in literature and poetry, but Nobel was also interested in social and peace-related issues. When Nobel died in 1896, his will specified that his fortune was to be used for prizes in peace, literature, medicine, physiology, chemistry, and physics. The Nobel Prizes are an extension of his lifelong interests.

Jean Sibelius (1865–1957)

Born in Hämeenlinna, Finland, from the age of fifteen Jean Sibelius focused on playing the violin. He attended school in Austria, Germany, and Finland, eventually abandoning his dream of being a violin virtuoso. In 1892 Sibelius married Aino Järnefeldt (sister of the well-known painter, Eero Järnefelt).

A prolific composer, Sibelius' works include well-known compositions such as *The Swan of Tuonela*, *Valse triste*, *Karelia Suite*, and *Finlandia* as well as music for a dozen plays, songs for piano and voice, choral music, the opera *Maiden in the Tower*, and a set of seven symphonies. Wagner was an early influence, but Sibelius' work was mostly influenced by Anton Bruckner, Ferruccio Busoni, and Tchaikovsky. Sibelius' primary rival was Gustav Mahler, but the two had little in common except that both were often inspired by folk music and literature.

Sibelius was inspired by nature, being very responsive to the seasons, to the "moods of nature," and to wildlife as well as to the sights, sounds, and smells from the Finnish landscape. He was also inspired by Finnish folk music, and the nature of Sibelius' orchestration has been compared to the Finnish character—"stripping away the superfluous."

To help celebrate Sibelius' ninetieth birthday, the Philadelphia Orchestra and Royal Philharmonic Orchestra performed his music in Finland. Later, conductors Eugene Ormandy and Sir Thomas Beecham met with Sibelius in his home; photographs of that meeting were included with albums of Sibelius' music released by EMI and Columbia Records in the United States and the UK.

Finland gained independence during his most

productive period, and Sibelius' music is credited with playing an important role in the development of a Finnish national identity. Before adopting the Euro, Sibelius' image was prominent on Finnish currency (100 mark note) and Finland's Flag Day is December 8, Sibelius' birthday. After his death, Sibelius' home, Ainola at Lake Tuusula, was sold to the State of Finland, and a museum was opened there in 1974.

Johanna Sigurdardottir (1942–)

Born in 1942 in Reykjavik, Johanna Sigurdardottir studied at the Commercial College of Iceland before becoming a flight attendant and office worker for the forerunner of Icelandair. Early in her career she was active in labor organizations, and in 1978 she ran for and was elected as a Social Democrat to the *Althing* (Icelandic Parliament). Sigurdardottir became Deputy Speaker of the *Althing* in 1979 and held that position again in 1983 and 1984. She was Minister of Social Affairs several times, and again held a ministerial position in the *Althing* after the election of 2007.

From 2003 to 2008, led by a small group of men who were influenced by developments in the United States, Iceland and Icelanders engaged in a frenzy of financial speculation. Home prices tripled and stock prices multiplied nine times, until October 2008 when the bubble burst.

The biggest banks went bankrupt, peoples' investments evaporated, and Icelanders were not happy. Following months of popular protests, the prime minister resigned and in his place Johanna Sigurdardottir was picked as the new Prime Minister of Iceland effective February 2009. This was a severe crisis, and a compelling reason to choose

Sigurdardottir was that she enjoyed more public confidence than almost any other member of parliament—she had been reelected eight times.

In 2002 Sigurdardottir had been joined in a civil union with Jonina Leosdottir, and they married in 2010 when same-sex marriage became legal in Iceland.

Sigrid Undset (1882–1949)

Born in Denmark, at age two Sigrid Undset moved with her family to Norway where she grew up in Christiana (Oslo). Her father's death when she was eleven ended Undset's hope of attending the university.

She completed a secretarial course and found employment in that field. At age sixteen she started writing fiction, but her first novel about life in the Middle Ages was rejected by publishers. She switched to writing love stories set in contemporary Oslo, and these were published and sold well.

The income from her books and a writer's scholarship allowed Undset to travel extensively, including living briefly in London and Rome. A Catholic, Undset was openly critical of the contemporary women's emancipation movement.

In 1919 Undset moved to Lillehammer, built her home, Bjerkebæk, and began writing *Kristin Lavransdatter*. This historical novel was set in Middle Ages Norway; life is realistically—not romantically—portrayed, and the central character is a woman. Undset's *Kristin Lavransdatter* trilogy was highly popular with Americans, and a Norwegian movie based on the first book was also popular here; at a screening in Minneapolis attended by this writer, many people were turned away.

She continued writing including *The Master of Hestviken* (four volumes in English), but mostly in recognition of *Kristin Lavransdatter*, Sigrid Undset was awarded the Nobel Prize in Literature in 1926. On January 25, 1940, Unset donated her Nobel Prize to Finland in support of its efforts in the Winter War.

Undset had been an early critic of the Nazis, and her books had been banned in Nazi Germany. Knowing that she would be arrested, Undset fled to Sweden when Norway was invaded. Her eldest son, a second lieutenant in the Norwegian Army, was killed in action a few kilometers from Bjerkebæk.

Raoul Wallenberg (1912–1947?)

Raoul Wallenberg was born in 1912 into an upper-class Swedish family that was involved in banking, diplomacy, academia, etc. His father died before Wallenberg was born, and he was raised by his mother and grandmother. Wallenberg's paternal grandfather became a mentor, and letters from the grandson to Gustaf Wallenberg, *Letters and Dispatches 1924–1944*, are a rich source of information about Raoul.

Because of the value of being exposed to new and different ideas, in the early 1930s Wallenberg traveled extensively in the United States and earned a degree in architecture at the University of Michigan. After graduation Wallenberg worked as a businessman in South Africa and in the Middle East before returning to live in Sweden. Letters from this period reveal a young man who responded calmly and self-confidently in difficult situations.

In Sweden, Wallenberg could not practice architecture

with his American degree and he was unsure of where his career was headed. When he was offered a "diplomatic" post during World War II, he accepted without hesitation. The Swedish government, which had diplomatic relations with Nazi Germany, realized that Hungary's Jews were in a precarious position; Wallenberg's assignment was, while pretending to be a diplomat, to do what he could to save Hungarian Jews.

In Budapest, with help from Carl-Ivan Danielsson and Per Ånger, Wallenberg expanded a ruse started by Ånger: issuing fake documents to Jews giving them the same protection as if they were Swedish citizens. Wallenberg's adversary in this work was Adolph Eichmann. Wallenberg's efforts were facilitated by his ability to function calmly and efficiently in very dangerous circumstances.

With help from others, Wallenberg directly and indirectly saved the lives of 100,000 Hungarian Jews. Today, Raoul Wallenberg is an honorary citizen of the United States, Canada, Hungary, and Israel. There are streets named after him as well as statues and memorials in numerous locations.

Acknowledgement

Steven Flink and John Schlagel read and edited the original manuscript. Without expressing either approval or disapproval, each offered suggestions that significantly improved the final edition. Marilyn McGriff provided cultural insight. Dave Sheppard provided sources for Corporate Social Responsibility. Other writers, the sources, are the foundation of this effort. Writings by Emmanuel Todd and Marc Bloch, together with essays in *Culture Matters, Resistance, Representation, and Community* and *Northern Revolts*, inspired and nurtured the central argument presented in these pages: Nordic countries excel at progress because of persistent culture. Linda edited and re-edited numerous versions; without her help and support this book would have been impossible.

Selected Bibliography

In addition to specific references, the following periodicals are generally valuable sources of information about Nordic culture: *Church and Life, The Danish Pioneer, The Finnish American Reporter, Nordstjernan, Norwegian American Weekly, The Quarterly, Swedish American Genealogist.*

Ahlstrom, Louis J. *Historical Sketches: Fifty-Five Years in Western Wisconsin 1869–1924.* Frederic, WI, 2010.

Anonymous. *The King's Mirror.* New York, 1917.

Appel, Charlotte. *Læsning og bogmarked i 1600-tallets Danmark.* Copenhagen, 2001.

Aruz, Joan. Farkas, Ann. Alekseev, Andrei. Korolkova, Elena. Editors. *The Golden Deer of Eurasia.* New York, 2000.

Baring, Maurice. *What I Saw in Russia.* London, 1927.

Bately, Janet. "Ohthere and Wulfstan in the Old English *Orosius,*" and "Text and Translation . . ." *Ohthere's Voyages: A Late 9th Century Account of Voyages along the Coasts of Norway and Denmark and Its Cultural Context.* Roskilde, 2007.

Birket-Smith, Kaj. *The Paths of Culture.* Madison, WI, 1965.

Blegen, Theodore C. *Norwegian Migration to America: 1825–1860*. New York, 1969.

Blickle, Peter. "Conclusions." *Resistance, Representation, and Community*. New York, 1997.

Blickle, Peter. Ellis, Steven. Österberg, Eva. "The Commons and the State: Representation, Influence, and the Legislative Process." *Resistance, Representation, and Community*. New York, 1997.

Bloch, Marc. *Feudal Society*. Chicago, 1961.

Bloch, Marc. *French Rural History: An Essay on its Basic Characteristics*. Berkeley, CA, 1984.

Borish, Steven M. *The Land of the Living: The Danish Folk High Schools and Denmark's Non-Violent Path to Modernization*. Grass Valley, CA, 1991.

Brace, Charles Loring. *The Norse-Folk*. New York, 1859.

Britton, Claes. *Sverige & Svenskarna*. Stockholm, 2003.

Brizendine, Louann. *The Female Brain*. New York, 2006.

Brooks, David. *The Social Animal: The Hidden Sources of Love, Character, and Achievement*. New York, 2011.

Brown, Nancy Marie. *The Far Traveler: Voyages of a Viking Woman*. Orlando, FL, 2007.

Burenhult, Göran. *Länkar till Vår Forntid: -en introduktion i Sveriges arkeologi*. Stockholm, 1988.

Carlsson, Sten; Rosen, Jerker; et al. *Den Svenska Historien*. Stockholm, 1992.

Cavalli-Sforza, Luigi Luca. *Genes, Peoples, and Languages*. New York, 2000.

Chaffee, John. *Thinking Critically*. Boston, 2003.

Chomsky, Noam. *The Architecture of Language*. New Delhi, 2000.

Cohen, Warren. *Ethics in Thought and Action*. New York, 1995.

Daun, Åke. *Swedish Mentality*. University Park, PA, 1996.

de Tocqueville, Alexis. *Democracy in America*. New York, 1969.

Dorfman, Joseph. *Thorstein Veblen and His America*. New York, 1934.

Eklof, Ben. *Russian Peasant Schools: Officialdom, Village Culture, and Popular Pedagogy, 1861–1914*. Berkeley, CA, 1990.

Engellau, Patrik. Henning, Ulf. Editors. *Nordic Views and Values*. Stockholm, 1984.

Etounga-Manguelle, Daniel. "Does Africa Need a Cultural Adjustment Program?" Harrison. *Culture Matters*. New York, 2000.

Forhoohar, Rana. "What Ever Happened to Upward Mobility?" *TIME Magazine*. Nov. 14, 2011.

Franck, Harry A. *A Scandinavian Summer: Some Impressions of Five Months in Denmark, Finland, Sweden, Norway, and Iceland*. New York, 1930.

Freuchen, Peter. *Vagrant Viking: My Life and Adventures*. New York, 1953.

Fridegård, Jan. *En Natt i Juli*. Trondheim, 1994.

Friedman, Milton. "The Social Responsibility of a Business Is to Increase Its Profits." *New York Times Magazine*. September 13, 1970.

Frykman, Jonas. "Sexual Intercourse and Social Norms: A Study of Illegitimate Births in Sweden 1831–1933." *Ethnologia Scandinavica*. Lund, 1975.

Fukuyama, Francis. "Social Capital." *Culture Matters*. New York, 2000.

Geertz, Clifford. *Works and Lives: The Anthropologist as Author.* Palo Alto, CA, 1988.

Gentile, Mary C. *Giving Voice to Values.* New Haven, CT, 2010.

Gjerde, Jon. "The "Would-Be Patriarch" and the "Self-Made Man." *On Distant Shores: Proceedings of the Marcus Lee Hansen Immigration Conference, Aalborg, Denmark 1992.* Aalborg, 1993.

Gjovig, Bruce. Opstad, Steinar. "Norway's Contribution to the United States and the World." *The Norseman.* Oslo, September 2006.

Glob, P.V. *The Mound People.* Ithaca, NY, 1970.

Gould, Stephen Jay. *Dinosaur in a Haystack.* New York, 1995.

Grondona, Mariano. "A Cultural Typology of Economic Development." *Culture Matters.* New York, 2000.

Gundersden, Paul. *Incorrigibly Independent: A Finnish Life.* Caux, 1999.

Gustafsson, Astrid. "Livet på Sollerön under vikingatiden." *Sool-Öen 2011: Solleröns hembygdsbok.* Mora, Sweden, 2011.

Gustafsson, Harold. "The Nordic Countries, so Similar and Yet so Different." *Northern Revolts: Medieval and Early Modern Peasant Unrest in the Nordic Countries.* Helsinki, 2004.

Hachmann, Rolf. *The Germanic People.* Geneva, 1971.

Handy, Charles. *The Hungry Spirit: Beyond Capitalism: A Quest for Purpose in the Modern World.* New York, 1998.

Harrison, Lawrence. *The Central Liberal Truth.* New York, 2006.

Harrison, Lawrence E. "Promoting Progressive Cultural Change." *Culture Matters.* New York, 2000.

Harrison, Lawrence E. Huntington, Samuel P. *Culture Matters: How Values Shape Human Progress.* New York, 2000.

Haskins, Charles Homer. *The Normans in European History.* Boston, 1915.

Herodotus. Strassler, Robert B. Editor. *The Landmark Herodotus: The Histories.* New York, 2007.

Hoglund, A. William. *Finnish Immigrants in America 1880–1920.* Madison, WI, 1960.

Hosking, Geoffrey. *Russia and the Russians: A History.* Cambridge, MA, 2001.

Huck, Barbara. *Exploring the Fur Trade Routes of North America.* Winnipeg, 2001.

Ibsen, Joy. "The Legacy of the Danish Resistance in World War II." *Danish-North American Relations since World War II.* Ames, IA, 2004.

Ibsen, Joy. "Songs of Denmark, Songs to Live By: Cultural Values Expressed in Traditional Danish Music." *Danish Culture, Past and Present: The Last Two Hundred Years.* Ames, IA 2006.

Icelandic sagas. *Havamal: The Sayings of the Vikings.* Reykjavik, 1992.

Icelandic sagas. *Heimskringla: History of the Kings of Norway.* Austin, TX, 1991.

Icelandic sagas. *The Sagas of the Icelanders.* London, 2000.

Imsen, Steinar. Vogler, Günter. "Communal Autonomy and Peasant Resistance in Northern and Central Europe." *Resistance, Representation, and Community.* New York, 1997.

Ingelman-Sundberg, Catharina. *Boken om Vikingarna.* Stockholm, 2004.

Inglehart, Ronald. "Culture and Democracy." *Culture Matters: How Values Shape Human Progress.* New York, 2000.

Inglehart, Ronald. Basanez, Miguel. Moreno, Aldejandro. Editors. *Human Values and Beliefs: A Cross-Cultural Sourcebook.* Ann Arbor, MI, 2001.

Inglehart, Ronald. Basanez, Miguel. Diez-Medrano, Jaime. Halman, Loek. Luijkx, Ruud. Editors. *Human Beliefs and Values: A Cross-Cultural Source Book Based on the 1999–2002 Values Surveys.* Mexico City, 2004.

Ipsen, Anne. "Three Tales of Two Towns." *Danish Culture Past and Present.* Ames, IA, 2006.

Jansson, Sven. *Runes in Sweden.* Stockholm, 1987.

Jenkins, David. *Sweden and the Price of Progress.* New York, 1968.

Johansson, Kenneth. "'The Lords from the Peasants or the Peasants from the Lords.'" *Northern Revolts: Medieval and Early Modern Peasant Unrest in the Nordic Countries.* Helsinki, 2004.

Jonassen, Christen T. *Values and Beliefs: A Study of American and Norwegian College Students.* Oslo, 1972.

Jones, Gwyn. *A History of the Vikings.* New York, 1984.

Juliusson, Arni Daniel. "Peasant Unrest in Iceland." *Northern Revolts: Medieval and Early Modern Peasant Unrest in the Nordic Countries.* Helsinki, 2004.

Katajal, Kimmo. "Conclusions." *Northern Revolts: Medieval and Early Modern Peasant Unrest in the Nordic Countries.* Helsinki, 2004.

Katajal, Kimmo. "For the King, Farms and Justice." *Northern Revolts: Medieval and Early Modern Peasant Unrest in the Nordic Countries.* Helsinki, 2004.

Katajala, Kimmo. "The Changing Face of Peasant Unrest in Early Modern Finland." *Northern Revolts: Medieval and Early Modern Peasant Unrest in the Nordic Countries.* Helsinki, 2004.

Keillor, Steven J. *Cooperative Commonwealth.* St. Paul, MN, 2000.

Kellogg, Robert. "Introduction." *The Sagas of the Icelanders.* London, 2000.

Kero, Reino. *Migration from Finland to North America . . .* Turku, Finland, 1974.

Klein, Joel I. & Rice, Condoleezza, chairs. *Independent Task Force Report No. 68: U.S. Education Reform and National Security.* New York, 2012.

Klindt-Jensen, Ole. *Denmark: Before the Vikings.* London, 1962.

Knipping, Mark. *Finns in Wisconsin.* Madison, WI, 1977.

Korpiola, Mia. "Swedish Medieval and Early Modern Treason Legislation." *Northern Revolts: Medieval and Early Modern Peasant Unrest in the Nordic Countries.* Helsinki, 2004.

Kristiansen, Kristian. *Europe before History.* Cambridge, UK, 2002.

Kristiansen, Kristian; Jensen, Jorgen. *Europe in the First Millennium B.C.* Sheffield, UK, 1994.

Landes, David. "Culture Makes Almost All the Difference." *Culture Matters.* New York, 2000.

Legg, Stuart. *The Barbarians of Asia: The Peoples of the Steppes from 1600 B.C.* New York, 1990.

Lewis, Michael. *Boomerang: Travels in the New Third World.* New York, 2011.

Lindström, Varpu. *Defiant Sisters: A Social History of Finnish Immigrant Women in Canada.* Toronto, 1992.

Linna, Väinö. *The Unknown Soldier.* Finland, 1991.

Lintelman, Joy K. *I Go to America: Swedish American Women and the Life of Mina Anderson.* St. Paul, MN, 2009.

Lipset, Seymour Martin. *American Exceptionalism: A Double-Edged Sword.* New York, 1996.

Lipset, Seymour Martin. Lenz, Gabriel Salman. "Corruption, Culture, and Markets." *Culture Matters.* New York, 2000.

Löfgren, Orvar. "Family and Household among Scandinavian Peasants." *Ethnologia Scandinavica.* Lund, 1974.

Lönnrot, Elias. *The Kalevala.* Cumberland, RI, 2002.

Lyon, Bryce. "Foreword." Bloch, Marc. *French Rural History: An Essay on its Basic Characteristics.* Berkeley, CA, 1984.

Maagerø, Eva; Simonsen, Birte. Editors. *Norway Society and Culture.* Kristiansand, 2005.

Mannheim, Karl. *Ideology and Utopia.* New York, 1936.

Massie, Robert K. *Peter the Great: His Life and World.* New York, 1980.

McGoogan, Ken. *Fatal Passage: The Story of John Rae, The Arctic Hero Time Forgot.* New York, 2002.

Michaelsen, Karsten Kjer. "The Teenage Ambassadors . . ." *Danish-North American Relations Since World War II,* Ames, IA, 2004.

Michelsen, Peter; Rasmussen, Holger. *Danish Peasant Culture.* Copenhagen, 1955.

Moberg, Vilhelm. *A History of the Swedish People.* New York, 1989.

Morsing, Mette. Midttun, Atle. Palmås, Karl. "Corporate Social Responsibility in Scandinavia,"

Nansen, Fridtjof. *Farthest North.* New York, 1999.

Nelsen, Harvey. "A Cultural Change Model." Tampa, unknown.

Njåstad, Magne. "Resistance in the Name of the Law." *Northern Revolts: Medieval and Early Modern Peasant Unrest in the Nordic Countries.* Helsinki, 2004.

Norelius, Eric. *Early Life of Eric Norelius 1833–1862.* Rock Island, IL, 1934.

North, Dick. *The Lost Patrol: The Mounties' Yukon Tragedy.* Vancouver, 1995.

Odlund, Martin. *The Life of Knute Nelson.* Minneapolis, MN, 1926.

Officer, Charles and Page, Jake. *A Fabulous Kingdom: The Exploration of the Arctic.* New York, 2001.

Olsen, Magnus. *Farms and Fanes of Ancient Norway.* Cambridge, MA, 1928.

Ostergren, Robert C. *A Community Transplanted.* Madison, WI, 1988.

Ostler, Nicholas. *Empires of the Word.* New York, 2005.

Ostrom, Elinor. *Governing the Commons: The Evolution of Institutions for Collective Action.* New York, 1990.

Pederson, John. "A Lioness for Denmark?" Petersen, Peter L., editor. *Danish-North American Relations since World War II.* Ames, IA, 2004.

Persson, Magnus. *Coming Full Circle: Return Migration and the Dynamics of Social Mobility on the Bjäre Peninsula 1860–1930.* Lund, 2007.

Persson, Stefan. *Kungamakt och Bonderätt: Om Danska Kungar och Bönder i Riket och i Göinge Härad Ca 1525–1640.* Lund, 2005.

Porter, Michael E. "Attitudes, Values, Beliefs, and the Microeconomics of Prosperity." *Culture Matters.* New York, 2000.

Porter, Michael. Kramer, Mark. "Strategy & Society: The Link between Competitive Advantage and Corporate Social Responsibility." *Harvard Business Review.* December 2006.

Rasmussen, Janet E. *New Land, New Lives.* Seattle, WA, 1993.

Riegler, Claudius. "Scandinavian Migrants Images and . . ." *Distant Magnets: Expectations and Realities in the Immigrant Experience, 1840–1930.* New York, 1993.

Robbins, Paula. *The Travels of Peter Kalm.* New York, 2007.

Roesdahl, Else. *The Vikings.* London, 1991.

Rosander, Carl. *Den Nye Skolmästaren: En Hankbok För Allmän Medborgerlig Bildning I Alla Kunskapens Grenar.* Chicago, about 1900.

Sæmundsson, Matthias. "Foreword." *Havamal: The Sayings of the Vikings.* Reykjavik, 1992.

Sahlberg, Pasi. *Finnish Lessons: What Can the World Learn from Educational Change in Finland?* New York, 2011.

Sawyer, Birgit and Peter. *Medieval Scandinavia.* Minneapolis, MN, 1993.

Sehmsdorf, Henning. "Envy and Fear in Scandinavian Folk Tradition." *Ethnologia Scandinavica.* Lund, 1988.

Semmingsen, Ingrid. *Norway to America: A History of the Migration.* Minneapolis, MN, 1978.

Skoglund, Elizabeth R. *A Quiet Courage: Per Anger, Wallenberg's Co-Liberator of Hungarian Jews.* Grand Rapids, MI, 1997.

Spufford, Margaret. *Small Books and Pleasant Histories: Popular Fiction and Its Readership in Seventeenth Century England.* Athens, GA, 1982.

Storli, Inger. "Ohthere and His World—A Contemporary Perspective." *Ohthere's Voyages: A Late 9th Century Account of Voyages along the Coasts of Norway and Denmark and Its Cultural Context.* Roskilde, 2007.

Strand, Robert. "Culture & CSR: Embracing the Scandinavian Approach to CSR." *Børsen special series on Corporate Social Responsibility.* [unknown].

214

Sundbärg, Gustav. *Sweden: Its People and Its Industry.* Stockholm, 1904.

Tacitus, *The Agricola and Germany of Tacitus.* London, 1911.

Thomas, W.W. Jr. *Sweden and the Swedes.* Chicago, 1892.

Todd, Emmanuel. *The Making of Modern France.* Oxford, 1991.

Turner, Frederick Jackson. *The Frontier in American History.* New York, 1920.

Vilkuna, Asko. "The Tale of the Birch-Bark Strip." *Ethnologia Scandinavica.* Lund, Sweden, 1975.

Völsunga Saga. London, about 1890.

Unknown, *Beowulf.* New York, 2000.

Wallenberg, Rauol. *Letters and Dispatches 1924–1944.* New York, 1995.

Wasastjerna, Hans R. *History of the Finns in Minnesota.* New York Mills, MN, 1957.

Weber, Max. *The Protestant Ethic and the "Spirit" of Capitalism.* New York, 2002.

Weisner, Thomas S. "Culture, Childhood, and Progress in Sub-Sahara Africa." *Culture Matters.* New York, 2000.

Wells, Spencer. *Deep Ancestry: Inside the Genographic Project.* Washington, D.C., 2007.

Weatherford, Jack. *Genghis Khan and the Making of the Modern World.* New York, 2004.

Wilkinson, Richard. Pickett, Kate. *The Spirit Level: Why Greater Equality Makes Societies Stronger.* New York, 2010.

Williams, Robin M. Jr. *American Society: A Sociological Interpretation.* New York, 1970.

Wolfram, Herwig. *History of the Goths.* Berkeley, CA, 1990.

Wood, Betty. *The Origins of American Slavery: Freedom and Bondage in the English Colonies.* New York, 1997.

Woodham-Smith, Cecil. *The Great Hunger: Ireland 1845–1849.* New York, 1962.

Zinn, Howard. *A People's History of the United States.* London, 1980.

Notes

1   Gunnar Myrdal, *The Asian Drama: An Inquiry into the Poverty of Nations* (New York: Pantheon, 1968), pages 27–28. Lawrence E. Harrison, Samuel P. Huntington, *Culture Matters: How Values Shape Human Progress* (New York: Basic Books, 2000), page *xxv*. Lawrence E. Harrison, "Promoting Progressive Cultural Change," *Culture Matters*, page 302.

2   Joseph Dorfman, *Thorstein Veblen and His America* (New York: Viking Press, 1934), page 326.

3   Louann Brizendine, *The Female Brain* (New York: Morgan Road Books, 2006), pages 26–28, 110–11.

4   Ronald Inglehart, Miguel Basanez, Aldejandro Moreno, *Human Values and Beliefs: A Cross-Cultural Sourcebook* (Ann Arbor: University of Michigan Press, 2001), pages 4, 15, 17, 20. Harold Gustafsson, "The Nordic Countries, so Similar and Yet so different," *Northern Revolts: Medieval and Early Modern Peasant Unrest in the Nordic Countries*, Kimmo Katajal, editor (Helsinki: 2004), pages 19, 24, 26–29, 31. Mia Korpiola, "Swedish Medieval and Early Modern Treason Legislation," *Northern Revolts: Medieval and Early Modern Peasant Unrest in the Nordic Countries*, Kimmo Katajal, editor (Helsinki: 2004), page 251.

5   Inglehart et al., *Human Values*, pages 4, 15, 17, 20. Kristian Kristiansen, *Europe before History* (Cambridge University Press, 2002), page 22. Göran Burenhult, *Länkar till Vår Forntid: -en*

217

introduktion i Sveriges arkeologi (Stockholm,1988), page 234. P.V. Glob, *The Mound People*, trans. Joan Bulman (Ithaca, NY: Cornell University Press, 1970), page 119. Henning Sehmsdorf, "Envy and Fear in Scandinavian Folk Tradition." *Ethnologia Scandinavica* (Lund, Sweden: Royal Gustaf Adolph Academy, 1988), page 34. Janet E. Rasmussen, *New Land, New Lives* (Seattle: University of Washington Press, 1993), page 14. Inger Storli, "Ohthere and His World—A Contemporary Perspective," *Ohthere's Voyages: A Late 9th Century Account of Voyages along the Coasts of Norway and Denmark and Its Cultural Context* (Roskilde: Viking Ship Museum, 2007), page 86.

6   Magnus Persson, *Coming Full Circle: Return Migration and the Dynamics of Social Mobility on the Bjäre Peninsula 1860–1930* (Lund, Sweden: Dept. of History, Lund University, 2007), page 47.

7   Eva Maagerø and Birte Simonsen, editors, *Norway Society and Culture* (Kristiansand: Portal, 2005), page 26.

8   Herwig Wolfram, *History of the Goths*, trans. Thomas J. Dunlap (Berkeley: University of California Press, 1990), page 219. Kristian Kristiansen and Jorgen Jensen, *Europe in the First Millennium B.C.* (Sheffield, UK: J.R. Collins, 1994), page 24.

9   Clifford Geertz, *Works and Lives: The Anthropologist as Author* (Stanford, CA: Stanford University Press, 1988), page 140. Williams, *American Society*, pages 23–30. Steven M. Borish, *The Land of the Living: The Danish Folk High Schools and Denmark's Non-Violent Path to Modernization* (Grass Valley, CA: Blue Dolphin, 1991), page 21. Spencer Wells, *Deep Ancestry: Inside the Genographic Project* (Washington, D.C.: National Geographic, 2007), page 20 (Darwin). Bryce Lyon, "Foreword," Bloch, *French Rural*, pages x–xii. Stephen Jay Gould, *Dinosaur in a Haystack* (New York: Harmony Books, 1995), page 94.

10   //www.worldvaluessurvey.org

11   Chomsky, page 2 (scientific analysis).

12   Christen T. Jonassen, *Values and Beliefs: A Study of American and Norwegian College Students* (Oslo, Norway: Univesitetsforlaget, 1972), pages 83, 85.

13 Ronald Inglehart, "Culture and Democracy," Lawrence E. Harrison & Samuel P. Huntington, *Culture Matters: How Values Shape Human Progress* (New York: Basic Books, 2000), pages 80, 86. Thomas S. Weisner, "Culture, Childhood, and Progress in Sub-Sahara Africa," Harrison, *Culture Matters*, page 142. Matthias Sæmundsson, "Foreword," *Havamal: The Sayings of the Vikings*, trans. Björn Jonasson (Reykjavik: Gudrun, 1992), page 14. Bloch, *French Rural*, pages 1, 34, 48, 74, 76. Kaj Birket-Smith, *The Paths of Culture* (Madison: University of Wisconsin Press, 1965), page 42. Emmanuel Todd, *The Making of Modern France*, trans. Anthony Forster and Betty Forster (Oxford: Basil Blackwell, 1991), page 61. Harvey Nelsen, "A Cultural Change Model." Tampa: University of Southern Florida. Peter Michelsen and Holger Rasmussen, *Danish Peasant Culture* (Copenhagen: Danish Folk Museum, 1955), pages 7–10. Borish, *Land of the Living*, page 80. Joy Ibsen, "The Legacy of the Danish Resistance in World War II," *Danish-North American Relations since World War II* (Ames, Iowa: The Danish American Heritage Society, 2004), page 36. John Pederson, "'A Lioness for Denmark'?—Ambassador Eugenie Anderson and Danish American Relations," *Danish-North American Relations since World War II* (Ames, IA: Danish American Heritage Society, 2004), page 48.

14 Williams, *American Society*, page 24.

15 Karl Mannheim, *Ideology and Utopia,* trans. Louis Wirth, Edward A. Shils (New York: Harcourt, Brace & World, 1936), page 84.

16 Lee M. Hollander, "Introduction," Snorri Sturluson, *Heimskringla: History of the Kings of Norway,* trans. Lee M. Hollander, (Austin: University of Texas Press, 1991), pages xix–xx.

17 David Jenkins, *Sweden and the Price of Progress* (New York: Coward-McCann, 1968), page 205.

18 Peter Blickle, "Conclusions," *Resistance, Representation, and Community,* editor Peter Blickle (New York: Oxford University Press, 1997), pages 337–38. Borish, *Land of the Living*, pages 13, 19, 121, 124, 134, 141, 179, 204, 289. Ben Eklof, *Russian Peasant Schools: Officialdom, Village Culture, and Popular Pedagogy,*

1861–1914 (Berkeley: University of California Press, 1990), pages 3–5, 8, 9. Birket-Smith, *Paths of Culture*, page 44. Bloch, *French Rural*, pages 199, 218. Persson, *Coming Full Circle*, page 231. Elinor Ostrom, *Governing the Commons: The Evolution of Institutions for Collective Action* (New York: Cambridge University Press, 1990), page 58. Richard Wilkinson and Kate Pickett, *The Spirit Level: Why Greater Equality Makes Societies Stronger* (New York: Bloomsbury, 2010), pages 238–39. Jenkins, *Sweden and the Price of Progress*, page 204 (Lis Asklund).

19   Eklof, *Russian Peasant Schools*, pages 3–5, 8, 9, 36, 37.

20   Harrison, *Culture*, page *xiv*. Ronald Inglehart, Loek Halman, and Christian Welzel, "Introduction," *Human Beliefs and Values: A Cross-Cultural Source Book Based on the 1999–2002 Values Surveys* (Mexico City: 2004), page 19. Alexis de Tocqueville, *Democracy in America* (New York: Doubleday Anchor, 1969), page 301. Wilkinson and Pickett, pages 238–39.

21   C.F. Nielsen, "Leipzig, October 9, 1989," *Church and Life*, Joy Ibsen, editor (Askov, MN: Nov. 15, 2009), Vol. LIX, pages 7–8.

22   Howard Zinn, *A People's History of the United States* (London: Longman, 1980), pages 435–59.

23   Arni Daniel Juliusson, "Peasant Unrest in Iceland," *Northern Revolts: Medieval and Early Modern Peasant Unrest in the Nordic Countries*, Kimmo Katajal, editor (Helsinki: 2004), pages 130–31, 140, 144–46.

24   Geoffrey Hosking, *Russia and the Russians: A History* (Cambridge, MA: Belkamp Press, 2001), pages 38–39.

25   The *Russian Primary Chronicle* states that the Rus were invited to rule. It matters not whether this was literally true; the significance is that it made sense that *a ruler was necessary*.

26   Jonassen, *Values and Beliefs*, page 13. Harrison, *Culture Matters*, pages xxv, xxvii–iii. David Landes, "Culture Makes Almost All the Difference," Harrison, *Culture Matters*, page 2. Michael E. Porter, "Attitudes, Values, Beliefs, and the Microeconomics of Prosperity," *Culture Matters*, page 14. Weisner, *Culture Matters*, page 143. Robert B. Strassler, editor, trans. Andrea L. Purvis, *The Landmark Herodotus: The Histories* (New York: Pantheon Books,

2007), page xxi (Pindar). Ostrom, *Governing the Commons*, page 35 (norms), 88–89. Borish, *Land of the Living*, page 26 (Martinsen).

27 Borish, *Land of the Living*, pages 26, 341. Gunnar Myrdal, *The Asian Drama*, pages 27–28. Harrison, *Culture*, page 302. Gould, *Dinosaur*, page 94.

28 Harrison, *Culture Matters*, page *xxv*.

29 Lawrence Harrison, *The Central Liberal Truth* (2006), pages 94–95.

30 Maagerø and Simonsen, page 169. Louis J. Ahlstrom, *Historical Sketches: Fifty-Five Years in Western Wisconsin 1869–1924*, trans. Inger Berggren, Carolyn Wedin, Stefan Sylvander (Frederic, WI: 2010), page 18.

31 Barack Obama, *Dreams from My Father: A Story of Race and Inheritance* (New York: Three Rivers Press, 2004), page *x*.

32 Jina Moore, "In Recount of World's Poor, Some Surprises," *The Christian Science Monitor*, Volume 102, Issue 52, Nov. 22, 2010, page 14.

33 Ireland: Cecil Woodham-Smith, *The Great Hunger: Ireland 1845–1849* (New York: Penguin, 1962), pages 15–37. English homes: Paula Robbins, *The Travels of Peter Kalm* (New York: Fleischmanns, 2007), page 46. Homes in Sweden: Charles Loring Brace, *The Norse-Folk* (New York: Scribner, 1859), pages 259, 380–81 (renters), 418–19 (renters). Poverty: Harry A. Franck, *A Scandinavian Summer: Some Impressions of Five Months in . . .* (New York: Grosset & Dunlap, 1930), pages 75, 101, 158, 164. English children were sent away to work at a younger age than Danish children: Charlotte Appel, *Læsning og bogmarked i 1600-tallets Danmark* (Copenhagen: Museum Tusculanums Forlag, 2001), page 99.

34 Ahlstrom, *Historical Sketches*, page 28.

35 Food: Joy K. Lintelman, *I Go to America: Swedish American Women and the Life of Mina Anderson* (St. Paul: Minnesota Historical Society Press, 2009), page 13.

36 Finland: Selina Keränen, "Huutolaislapsi: at the mercy of others," *The Finnish American Reporter* (Hancock, MI: January 2011), page 9.

37   Brace, *The Norse-Folk*, page 260.

38   *Den Nye Skolmästaren: En Hankbok För Allmän Medborgerlig Bildning I Alla Kunskapens Grenar* (Chicago: Svenska Amerikanarens Förlag, about 1900), page 503. This book is probably a reprint of Carl Rosander's *Den Kunskapsrike Skolmästern, Eller Huf...*, first published about 1860 in Stockholm. *Den Nye Skolmästern* does not list either a publication date or an author, but, printed on the bottom of page one, in the form of a footnote is, "1.—*Rosander*, Skolmästern." Rosander died in 1877. A similar (not identical) chart was included in Gustav Sundbärg, editor, *Sweden, Its People and Its Industry* (Stockholm: Norstedt, 1904), page 137.

39   Robbins, *Travels*, page 47.

40   Birket-Smith, *Paths of Culture*, pages 247, 243–44.

41   Strassler, *Herodotus. The Golden Deer of Eurasia,* Joan Aruz, Ann Farkas, Andrei Alekseev, Elena Korolkova, editors (New York: Yale University Press, 2000), see index.

42   Wolfram, *Goths*, pages 19–26, 381 (note 78). One of the Icelandic sagas, *Ynglings saga*, describes a migration from north of the Black Sea to the Nordic region. According to this saga, Danish royalty were Sköldunger while the Scythians of Herodotus time called themselves Skoloti. Sailing the European west coast in fourth century B.C., Pytheas of Massalia (a Greek) visited an amber-producing area up north that he called "Scythia" (apparently the west coast of Denmark). In the Old Norse language the name for central Sweden was "*Svíþjóth*," and "*store-Svíþjóth*" was Scythia north of the Black Sea (*store* means "great"). E.C. Otte, *Scandinavian History* (London: McMillan, 1874), pages 19–23. Leiv Heggstad, *Gamalnorsk Ordbok* (Oslo: Det Norske Samlaget, 1930), pages 679, 676, 722. Janet Bately, "Ohthere and Wulfstan in the Old English *Orosius,*" and "Text and Translation . . .," *Ohthere's Voyages: A Late 9th Century Account of Voyages along the Coasts of Norway and Denmark and Its Cultural Context* (Roskilde: Viking Ship Museum, 2007), pages 18–19, 34, 40. Sturluson, "Saga of the Ynglings," *Heimskringla, trans. Hollander,*

pages 6 (note 2), 13, 15. Fridtjof Nansen, *In Northern Mists*, Vol. I, page 99 (Scythia on the Baltic). Skald Sigvat referred to Sweden circa A.D. 1020 as "Svitjod" (*Heimskringla:* "St. Olaf's saga"). Stuart Legg, *The Barbarians of Asia, The Peoples of the Steppes from 1600 B.C.* (New York: Dorset, 1990), pages 63, 69, 71. The Latin word *Scythae* (Scythians) meant all of the nomadic tribes living north of the Black and Caspian seas. Barry Cunliffe, *The Extraordinary Voyage of Pytheas the Greek* (New York: Penguin, 2002), pages 146–47. E.V. Gordon, *An Introduction to Old Norse,* second revised edition by A.R. Taylor (Oxford: Clarendon Press, 1986), pages 26, 251.

43 Kristiansen, *Before*, page 285. Wells, *Deep Ancestry*, pages 224–25. Ole Klindt-Jensen, *Denmark: Before the Vikings* (London: Thames and Hudson, 1962), page 123. Burenhult, *Länkar*, pages 152, 234. Aruz et al., *Golden Deer*, page 19.

44 Herodotus, *Histories*, Book IV, Chapter 26.

45 Herodotus, *Histories*, Book IV, Chapter 116. M. Rostovtzeff, *Iranians & Greeks in South Russia* (New York: Russell, 1922), pages 33–34 ("[Sarmatian] female sovereigns, female warriors") Legg, *Barbarians of Asia*, page 69. Tadeusz Sulimirski, *The Sarmatians* (Great Britain: Thames and Hudson, 1970), pages 22–23, 33–34, 66, 105. Female graves at Pokrovka (Kazakhstan) contain warrior gear. Sarmatian women ceased being warriors when they married, see Brynhild in *Völsunga Saga,* Magnusson and Morris translators (London: Walter Scott, ?1890), 70. Kristiansen, *Before*, 285.

46 Aruz et al., *Golden Deer*, page 4. Glob, *Mound*, pages 35, 44–45. *Östergötland: En läsbok om hembygged* (Malmö: Beyronds AB, 1974), 4th ed., page 28.

47 Rolf Hachmann, *The Germanic People,* trans. James Hogarth (Geneva: Nagel, 1971), 70–72.

48 Burenhult, *Länkar*, page 152. Birgit and Peter Sawyer, *Medieval Scandinavia* (Minneapolis: University of Minnesota Press, 1993), page 166. *Britannica* (2002) 15th Ed., Vol. 11, page 487.

49 Burenhult, *Länkar*, page 152.

50   Varpu Lindström, *Defiant Sisters: A Social History of Finnish Immigrant Women in Canada* (Toronto: 1992), page 9.

51   "Helsingin Sanomat," *The Finnish American Reporter* (Hancock, MI: June 2010), page 20 (FIMM genetic evidence).

52   Bo Pederby, *Libers Historiska Atlas* (Viborg, DK: 2005), page 11.

53   Alfred Church and William Brodribb trans., *The Agricola and Germany of Tacitus* (London: Macmillan, 1911), page 93.

54   *Tacitus*, 1911, page 101.

55   Carolyn Dewald, "On Women and Marriage in Herodotus," Robert B. Strassler, editor, trans. Andrea L. Purvis, *The Landmark Herodotus: The Histories* (New York: Pantheon Books, 2007), Appendix U, pages 838–42.

56   *Völsunga*, 76–77. Catharina Ingelman-Sundberg, *Boken om Vikingarna* (Stockholm: Prisma, 2004), pages 220–21, 232–33. Sten Carlsson, Jerker Rosen, et al., *Den Svenska Historien* (Stockholm: Bonnier, 1992), Book One, page 185. Norrman, "Nordic Oral Tradition," *ASI Posten*, Vol. 25, No. 3, page 4.

57   Astrid Gustafsson, "Livet på Sollerön under vikingatiden," *Sool-Öen 2011: Solleröns hembygdsbok* (Sollerö Hembygdsförening), page 11. Bruce Gjovig, Steinar Opstad, "Norway's Contribution to the United States and the World," *The Norseman* (Oslo: September 2006), pages 18–19.

58   Örnolfur Thorsson, editor, *The Sagas of the Icelanders* (London: Penguin, 2000), pages 270, 274, 303, 332 (Viking wife to control the finances and have half the estate).

59   Nancy Marie Brown, *The Far Traveler: Voyages of a Viking Woman* (Harcourt, 2007), pages 60 (Carol Glover), 66.

60   Ingelman-Sundberg, *Boken om Vikingarna*, pages 202–05. Gjovig and Opstad, pages 18–19.

61   Marc Bloch, *Feudal Society*, trans. L.A. Manyon (Chicago: University of Chicago Press, 1961), pages 136–38.

62   Bloch, *French Rural*, pages 151–51, 158, 164–65. Hosking, *Russia*, pages 48, 67–68, 227, 295. Bloch, *Feudal*, pages 136–38.

63   Brown, *Far Traveler*, pages 252–53. Ingelman-Sundberg, *Boken om Vikingarna*, page 209.

64   Johannes Althusius, *Politica* (1603), Chapters II–III.

65   Barbara Tuchman, *A Distant Mirror* (New York: Ballantine Books, 1979), page 211.

66   Magne Njåstad, "Resistance in the Name of the Law," *Northern Revolts: Medieval and Early Modern Peasant Unrest in the Nordic Countries*, Kimmo Katajal, editor (Helsinki: 2004), 97–98, 114–15. Kimmo Katajal, "Conclusions," *Northern Revolts: Medieval and Early Modern Peasant Unrest in the Nordic Countries*, Kimmo Katajal, editor (Helsinki: 2004), page 262. Vilhelm Moberg, *A History of the Swedish People, II*, trans. Paul Austin (New York: Dorset Press, 1989), pages 199–200.

67   Sawyer, *Medieval Scandinavia*, page 172.

68   Orvar Löfgren, "Family and Household among Scandinavian Peasants," *Ethnologia Scandinavica* (Lund: Royal Gustav Adolph Academy, 1974), 30–38. Jonas Frykman, "Sexual Intercourse and Social Norms: A Study of Illegitimate Births in Sweden 1831–1933." *Ethnologia Scandinavica* (Lund: Royal Gustav Adolph Academy, 1975), pages 110–47. Sawyer, *Medieval Scandinavia*, page 172. Brown, *Far Traveler*, page 252. Lindström, *Defiant Sisters*, pages 78–79, 80–82, 103. Catholic view: Todd, *Making of Modern France*, pages 92–93.

69   Maagerø and Simonsen, page 50.

70   Maagerø and Simonsen, page 50. P. Ryden, *En Dalason* (Chicago: Martensons, 1914), pages 86–87. John Cederoth, editor, *Något om Separatismen och Baptismen* (Sundsvall: Vesterlunds, 1885), pages 49, 53, 58, 65–66.

71   *Något om Separatismen*, page 17.

72   Kenneth Johansson, "'The Lords from the Peasants or the Peasants from the Lords,'" *Northern Revolts: Medieval and Early Modern Peasant Unrest in the Nordic Countries*, Kimmo Katajal, editor (Helsinki: 2004), 81–82, 54, 79.

73   Sundbärg, *Sweden*, page 274.

74   Selina Keränen, "An Inside Look at Finnish Politics," *The Finnish American Reporter* (Hancock, MI: November, 2010), page 21.

75   Gjovig and Opstad, pages 18–19.

76   Michelsen and Rasmussen, page 11.

77   Birket-Smith, *Paths of Culture*, pages 243–44 (matrilineal) 247.

78 Brizendine, various.

79 Robert Strand, "Culture and CSR: Embracing the Scandinavian Approach to CSR," *Børsen Special Series on Corporate Social Responsibility*, pages 2–3, rs.ikl@cbs.dk. Åke Daun, *Swedish Mentality* (University Park: Pennsylvania State University Press, 1996), pages 74–78, 86, 142–43, 204.

80 Elizabeth R. Skoglund, *A Quiet Courage: Per Anger, Wallenberg's Co-Liberator of Hungarian Jews* (Grand Rapids, MI: Baker Books, 1997), page 141.

81 Rasmussen, *New Land*, page 115

82 Birket-Smith, *Paths of Culture*, page 246 (Njal).

83 Sawyer, *Medieval Scandinavia*, pages 167–68. Magnus Olsen, *Farms and Fanes of Ancient Norway*, trans. Th. Gleditsch (Cambridge, MA: Harvard University Press, 1928), pages 42–55.

84 France, communal living: Bloch, *French Rural*, pages 164–65. Luigi Luca Cavalli-Sforza, *Genes, Peoples, and Languages*, trans. Mark Seielstad (New York: North Point Press, 2000), pages 184–85. Todd, *Making of Modern France*, pages 15, 68–69. Jack Goody, *The Development of the Family and Marriage in Europe* (Cambridge: Cambridge University Press, 1994), pages 22, 235.

85 Hosking, *Russia*, page 17.

86 *Tacitus*, 1911, pages 99–103.

87 Bloch, *Feudal*, pages 154, 158.

88 Else Roesdahl, *The Vikings*, trans. Margeson and Williams (London: Penguin, 1991), page 61.

89 Sæmundsson, "Forword," page 14.

90 Maagerø and Simonsen, page 43.

91 Roesdahl, *The Vikings*, page 62.

92 Sturluson, *Heimskringla, trans. Hollander,* page 8.

93 Juliusson, *Revolts*, pages 130–31.

94 Juliusson, *Revolts*, page 146.

95 Sæmundsson, "Foreword," page 14.

96 Katajala, *Revolts*, pages 12, 14.

97 Roesdahl, *The Vikings*, pages 60-61. Ingelman-Sundberg, *Boken om Vikingarna*, 202–03, 205.

98   Sæmundsson, "Foreword," page 14.

99   Anonymous, *The King's Mirror*, trans. Laurence M. Larson (New York: Twayne, 1917), page 82.

100 Rasmussen, *New Land*, pages 115, 117, 133, 152, 169, 189, 205, 213–14, 241, 261, 265.

101 Hosking, *Russia*, page 222.

102 Bloch, *Feudal*, pages 123-25.

103 Lindström, *Defiant Sisters*, pages 9, 13.

104 Inglehart, *Human Beliefs*, question A025.

105 Berit Hessen, "New Film about the 'Child Wanderings' in Norway," *Norwegian American Weekly* (Seattle: July 10, 2009), page 12.

106 Katajala, *Revolts*, pages 12, 14. Charles Homer Haskins, *The Normans in European History* (Houghton Mifflin, 1915), 38–39. Aug. J. Thebaud, "History of Ireland," *Northmen in History* (Northfield, MN: Mohn Printing Co), pages 41, 29.

107 Jonassen, *Values and Beliefs*, pages 81–86. Seymour Martin Lipset and Gabriel Salman Lenz, "Corruption, Culture, and Markets," *Culture Matters*, pages 119–20. Eric Hoffer, *The True Believer: Thoughts on the Nature of Mass Movements* (New York: Harper and Row, 1951), page 37.

108 Franck, *Summer*, page 92.

109 Maagerø and Simonsen, page 174.

110 Sturluson, *Heimskringla*, trans. Hollander, page 11.

111 Nicholas Ostler, *Empires of the Word* (New York: Harper Collins, 2005), page 278.

112 Sven Jansson, *Runes in Sweden*, trans. Peter Foote (Sweden: Gidlunds, 1987), pages 165, 173, 175. Sawyer, *Medieval Scandinavia*, pages 10–11. Brown, *Far Traveler*, page 259. Gwyn Jones, *A History of the Vikings* (New York: Oxford University Press, 1984), rev. ed. pages 71, 73.

113 Anonymous, *Mirror*, page 81–83.

114 Njåstad, *Revolts*, pages 114–15. The Norwegian law was written in Old Norse, circa A.D. 1274.

115 Anne Ågotnes, editor, *Runer fra Bryggen og Andre Smakebiter fraa Samlingene* (Trondheim: Bryggens Museum, 1997), pages 1–14.

116 Asko Vilkuna, "The Tale of the Birch-Bark Strip," *Ethnologia Scandinavica* (Lund: Royal Gustav Adolph Academy, 1975), pages 73, 75.

117 Vilkuna, "Birch-Bark," pages 73, 75.

118 Ingelman-Sundberg, *Boken om Vikingarna*, page 199.

119 Bloch, *Feudal*, pages 76–77, 79–81. Hosking, *Russia*, pages 206–09. Anonymous, *Mirror*, page 53.

120 Sundbärg, *Sweden*, page 137.

121 Jansson, *Runes in Sweden,* pages 173–75.

122 Kaarina Brooks [Alliston, Ontario], "Learning to read in 1543," *The Finnish American Reporter* (Hancock, MI: September 2010), page 9.

123 Hulda Magnusson, *Första Läseboken för Skolan och Hemmet* (Rock Island, IL: Augustana, 1908), page 43.

124 Lindström, *Defiant Sisters*, page 120. Brooks, "Learning," *FAP,* September 2010, page 9.

125 Maagerø and Simonsen, page 174.

126 Appel, *Læsning* page 249. (Egil Johansson in Graff: Literacy and Social Development, pages 155-82) Eklof, *Russian Peasant Schools*, pages 8, 9. Gary G. Erickson, "Today's Norwegian-Americans Challenged: Develop modern ways to relate to today's Norway," *Norwegian American Weekly* (Seattle: Aug. 28, 2009), pages 1, 13.

127 Appel, *Læsning*, pages 17–18.

128 Lloyd C. Hackl, *The Wooden Shoe People* (Center City, MN: 1986), page 25.

129 At Minnesota History Center: Emory Johnson, "Per Andersson's Letters from Chisago Lake." *The Swedish Pioneer Historical Quarterly*. Original letters in Gustavus Adolphus archives.

130 Appel, *Læsning*, pages 59–65.

131 Maagerø and Simonsen, page 16.

132 Lindström, *Defiant Sisters*, page 15.

133 Todd, *Making of Modern France*, page 136.

134 Margaret Spufford, *Small Books and Pleasant Histories: Popular Fiction and Its Readership in Seventeenth-Century England* (Athens: University of Georgia Press, 1982), 21. Appel, *Læsning*, page 99.

135 Eklof, *Russian Peasant Schools*, pages 3, 5.

136 Eklof, *Russian Peasant Schools*, pages 3, 5, 36–37, 67, 84. Also see Eklof page 106 (schools as a social control tool). While they were in control, the English would not allow the Irish to be educated: Woodham-Smith, *Hunger*, page 27. Before the American Civil War, it was illegal to educate slaves in the South.

137 <www.engtrends.com>

138 Michael Lewis, *Boomerang: Travels in the New Third World* (New York: W.W. Norton, 2011), pages 61–62. Mary C. Gentile, *Giving Voice to Values* (New Haven, CT: Yale University Press, 2010), pages 39-40. SAT & ACT: Frank Eltman "New Rules Such as Submitting Photo Come after Cheating Scandal" (Associated Press, March 2012), Mineola, NY.

139 Anonymous, *Mirror*, page 53. Robert Kellogg, "Introduction," Örnolfur Thorsson, ed., *The Sagas of the Icelanders* (London: Penguin, 2000), page *xxi*.

140 Appel, *Læsning*, page 249.

141 Pasi Sahlberg, *Finnish Lessons: What Can the World Learn from Educational Change in Finland?* (New York: Teachers College Press, 2011). Council on Foreign Relations: Joel I. Klein, Condoleezza Rice, chairs, *Independent Task Force Report No. 68: U.S. Education Reform and National Security* (New York: 2012), pages 24, 26–28. Erickson, "Today's Norwegian-Americans," pages 1, 13.

142 ". . . *stodo de alla sida vid sida, hög och låg, lärda och olärda, grosshandlare och bokhållare*" Harald Lundberg, *Sundsvalls Strejken* (Cewe-Förlaget, 1979), page 14.

143 Wilkinson and Pickett, pages 45–54. Common Pool Resources (CPR): Ostrom, *Governing the Commons*, pages 35, 88–89.

144 Cavalli-Sforza, *Genes,* pages 184–85.

145 Todd, *Making of Modern France*, pages 68–69. Lipset and Lenz, *Culture Matters*, page 119.

146 Gustafsson, *Revolts*, pages 29, 31.

147 Robert K. Massie, *Peter the Great: His Life and World* (New York: Knopf, 1980), pages 10–11.

148 Bloch, *Feudal*, pages 145–50.

149 Bloch, *Feudal,* pages 178, 49–50, 176–77.

150 Haskins, *Normans*, pages 27–28.

151 Rollo was a leader, a chieftain, but he could not order his men to do what he himself had refused to do—they were egalitarian.

152 Borish, *Land of the Living*, pages 120–22, 142. Anne Ipsen, "Three Tales of Two Towns," *Danish Culture Past and Present*, Linda M. Chementi and Birgit Flemming Larsen, editors (Ames, IA: 2006), pages 124–29.

153 Kellogg, "Introduction," page *xxxiv.*

154 Geertz, *Works and Lives*, page 140.

155 Hosking, *Russia*, pages 40-41. Maagerø and Simonsen, page 43.

156 W.W. Thomas, Jr., *Sweden and the Swedes* (Chicago: Rand, McNally, 1892), page 28.

157 Gustafsson, *Revolts*, pages 26–29, 31. Eric Norelius, *Early Life of Eric Norelius 1833–1862*, trans. Emeroy Johnson (Rock Island, IL: Augustana Book Concern, 1934), page 78. Hans R. Wasastjerna, *History of the Finns in Minnesota,* trans. Toivo Rosvall (New York Mills, MN: Northwest Publishing, 1957), page 53. Thomas, *Sweden*, pages 27–28.

158 Borish, *Land of the Living*, pages 142, 223, 237–38. Theodore C. Blegen, *Norwegian Migration to America: 1825–1860* (New York: Haskell House, 1969), page 5. Mark Knipping, *Finns in Wisconsin* (Madison: The State Historical Society of Wisconsin, 1977), page 11. Gerald F. Carlson, *Hometown Folks: A Finnish-American Saga* (St. Cloud, MN: North Star Press, 1997), 12, 24. *Något om*, 17 (women). Jan Fridegård, *En Natt i Juli* (Trondhjem, 1994), 8–9, 31 (A *statare* man stood up to his employer). A. William Hoglund, *Finnish Immigrants in America 1880–1920* (Madison: University of Wisconsin Press, 1960), page 146 (note

19). Lindström, *Defiant Sisters*, pages 11, 19, 31, 94–96, 98–99, 110, 128, 132, 137–40.

159 Borish, *Land of the Living*, pages 220–21. Maagerø and Simonsen, pages 14, 12. Sundbärg, *Sweden*, pages 138–39, 144, 157.

160 Brace, *The Norse-Folk*, page 286.

161 Väinö Linna, *The Unknown Soldier* Finland: 1991). Paul Gundersden, *Incorrigibly Independent: A Finnish Life* (Helsinki: Caux Books, 1999), pages 39–45.

162 George Keenan, reprint *Tent Life in Siberia* (Layton, UT: Gibbs Smith Inc., 1986), page 38. Massie, *Peter the Great*, pages 10–11.

163 Peter Freuchen, *Vagrant Viking: My Life and Adventures*, trans. Johan Hambro (New York: Messner, 1953), 352–53.

164 *Nansen in the Frozen World* (Chicago: Monroe Book Co., about 1897), page 193. Borish, *Land of the Living*, pages 125, 132, 210. Martin Odlund, *The Life of Knute Nelson* (Minneapolis: The Lund Press, 1926), page 319.

165 Maagerø and Simonsen, pages 169, 179.

166 Borish, *Land of the Living*, page 222 (Judith Hansen).

167 Wilkinson and Pickett.

168 Maagerø and Simonsen, page 43 (Vikings versus Christianity).

169 Hosking, *Russia*, page 202.

170 Bloch, *Feudal*, pages 123–25.

171 Sundbärg, *Sweden*, pages 144, 157.

172 Sahlberg, *Finnish Lessons*, page 10. Jonassen, *Values and Beliefs*, pages 83, 90. Wilkinson and Pickett, pages 196–97, 210–13.

173 Inglehart, *Human Beliefs*, question A032.

174 Harrison, *Truth*, page 162.

175 Strand, "Culture and CSR," pages 2–4.

176 Moberg, *History,* Volume II, page 192.

177 Robert C. Ostergren, *A Community Transplanted* (Madison: University of Wisconsin Press, 1988), page 90. Moberg, *History*, Vol. II, page 192.

178 Borish, *Land of the Living*, page 71.

179 Johansson, *Revolts*, page 79.

180 Steven J. Keillor, *Cooperative Commonwealth* (St. Paul: MHSP, 2000), pages 83, 140–42.

181   Johannes Althusius, *Politica* (1603), Chapter IX.

182   Norelius, *Early Life*, page 93. Brace, *The Norse-Folk*, pages 38–39, 267.

183   Borish, *Land of the Living*, page 13.

184   *Tacitus*, 1911, page 104. Legg, *Barbarians of Asia*, page 46. Wolfram, *Goths*, pages 11, 19, 379 (note 45), 381 (note 98).

185   *Hrafnkel's Saga & Other Stories*, trans. Hermann Palsson, from *Nordic Views and Values*, Engellau and Henning, editors (Stockholm: 1984), pages 65–69.

186   Brace, *The Norse-Folk*, pages 38–39, 267. No money turned in: David Dishneau, "Highway Cash Spill in MD Poses Ethical Dilemma," *The Arizona Republic* (March 24, 2012), page A8.

187   Ryden, *En Dalason*, pages 86–87. Elsa Lagevik, *The People of the Red Barns*, trans. Vicky Oliver, Gävle, Sweden: 1996), page 29.

188   O.N. Nelson, *History of the Scandinavians and Successful Scandinavians in the United States* (Minneapolis, MN: 1899), Vol. II, pages 4–10.

189   Inglehart, *Human Beliefs*.

190   Inglehart, *Culture Matters*, page 90. Francis Fukuyama, "Social Capital," Harrison, *Culture Matters*, pages 98–99. Lipset and Lenz, *Culture Matters*, pages 119, 122–23. Harrison, "Promoting," *Culture Matters*, page 299. Lewis, *Boomerang*, pages 54–55.

191   Sæmundsson, "Foreword," page 14.

192   Ibsen, "Resistance," page 39.

193   Maagerø and Simonsen, pages 168, 36. Sæmundsson, "Foreword," page 14. Sahlberg, *Finnish Lessons*, page 10. Jonathan Riikonen, "Those Peculiar, 'Un-Average' Finns," *The Finnish American Reporter* (Hancock, MI: Jan. 2010), page 6.

194   Borish, *Land of the Living*, page 71.

195   Gay & Laney Salisbury, *The Cruelest Miles* (New York: W.W. Norton, 2003), page 76.

196   Maagerø and Simonsen, pages 25, 30. Ostrom, *Governing the Commons*, page 108. Janey Smiley, "Preface," Örnolfur Thorsson, ed., *The Sagas of the Icelanders* (London: Penguin, 2000), page xii. Brown, *Far Traveler*, pages 111–12

197 Borish, *Land of the Living*, pages 316–17 (envy). Dr. Richard Andersen, "Danish Nooks and Crannies," *The Danish Pioneer* (Hoffman Estates, IL: Bertelsen, Oct. 26, 2009), Issue #22, page 6.

198 Bloch, *Feudal*, pages 88–93, 101.

199 Anders Fryxell, *History of Sweden*, trans. Anne von Schoultz (London: Schulze and Co., 1844), Part I, 9–10.

200 Jordanes, *The Gothic History of Jordanes in English Version*, trans. Charles Mierow (New York: Barnes and Noble, 1915), page 22. *Encyclopædia Britannica*, Otis Day Kellog, ed. (Chicago: The Werner Company, 1902), Vol. XIII, 748–49 ("Here we have in all probability a verbatim extract from Cassidorious, who has interwoven with his narrative large portions of the Gothic sagas.") *Britannica* (2002), Vol. 4, 885. A wood carving on a stave church at Hylestad, Norway; a rock carving near Eskilstuna (Ramsundsberget); and picture stones on Gotland, Sweden, depict scenes from *Völsunga*. Ingelman-Sundberg, *Boken om Vikingarna*, 220–21, 232–33. Carlsson, Book One, 131, 185. A tapestry circa A.D. 1000 from Jämtland depicting *Völsunga*, Lena Norrman, "Library Talk on Nordic Oral Tradition," *ASI Posten* (Minneapolis, MN 2006), Vol. 25, Nos. 3, 4.

201 Jordanes, *Gothic History*, pages 104–11.

202 *Völsunga*, 76–77. Ingelman-Sundberg, *Boken om Vikingarna*, pages 220–21, 232–33. Carlsson, Book One, 185. Norrman, "Nordic Oral Tradition."

203 Daun, *Swedish Mentality*, pages 135–42.

204 *The Saga of the Volsungs*, R.G. Finch trans. & ed., Chapter 22, pages 39–40.

205 Kellogg, "Introduction," pages *ix, xii.*

206 Juliusson, *Revolts*, pages 119, 122. Roesdahl, *The Vikings*, page 62. Kellogg, "Introduction," pages *ix, x, xi, xxi, xxix, xxxi*. Jones, *History of the Vikings*, pages 288–89.

207 Anonymous, *Mirror*, page 53.

208 Anonymous, *Mirror*, pages 79–81.

209 Anonymous, *Mirror*, pages 79–90.

210 Katajal, *Revolts*, page 262. Njåstad, *Revolts*, pages 114–15. Joy Ibsen, "Songs of Denmark, Songs to Live By: Cultural Values Expressed in Traditional Danish Music," Linda M. Chementi and Brigit Flemming Larsen, editors, *Danish Culture, Past and Present: The Last Two Hundred Years* (Ames, IA: The Danish American Heritage Society, 2006), page 364.

211 Bloch, *Feudal*, pages 76–77, 79–81.

212 Hosking, *Russia*, pages 99, 165, 170.

213 Bloch, *Feudal*, pages 74–75.

214 Samuel Jackson, editor, *The New Schaff-Herzog Encyclopedia of Religious Knowledge* (New York: Funk and Wagnalls), Vol. VII, page 355.

215 *Schaff-Herzog*, Vol. III, page 382.

216 *Schaff-Herzog*, Vol. IV, page 141.

217 Kimmo Katajal, "For the King, Farms and Justice," *Northern Revolts: Medieval and Early Modern Peasant Unrest in the Nordic Countries*, Kimmo Katajal, editor (Helsinki: 2004), page 206. Maagerø and Simonsen, page 47.

218 Anonymous, *Mirror*, pages 5, 11. Maagerø and Simonsen, page 66.

219 Maurice Baring, *What I Saw in Russia* (London: Heinemann, 1927), pages 20–21.

220 Robbins, *Travels*, pages 45, 95.

221 Franck, *Summer*, page 52.

222 Mariano Grondona, "A Cultural Typology of Economic Development," *Culture Matters*, page 51. Daniel Etounga-Manguelle, "Does Africa Need a Cultural Adjustment Program?," *Culture Matters*, page 69. Harrison, *Culture Matters*, page 299.

223 John Chaffee, *Thinking Critically* (Boston: Houghton Mifflin, 2003), seventh ed. pages 2–10. Borish, *Land of the Living*, page 313. Sundbärg, *Sweden*, page 139. Lintelman, *I Go to America*, page 119.

224 Landes, *Culture Matters*, pages 11–12.

225 Todd, *Making of Modern France*, page 175.

226 www2.elca.org/education/martinluther/

227   Sawyer, *Medieval Scandinavia*, page 172.

228   Brace, *The Norse-Folk*, pages 215–20.

229   Inglehart, *Human Beliefs*, 2004.

230   Kim Ode, "Norway: It's Good Enough for Us," *Star Tribune* (Minneapolis: Oct. 13, 2011), page E2.

231   Rasmussen, *New Land*, page 115.

232   Franck, *Summer*, page 99.

233   Bloch, *Feudal*, pages 74–75. Hosking, *Russia*, pages 165, 170.

234   Bloch, *Feudal*, pages 82–85. Hosking, *Russia*, pages 15, 40–41, 97–98.

235   Hosking, *Russia*, pages 40–41.

236   Keenan, *Siberia*, pages 395–96. Hosking, *Russia*, page 15.

237   Hosking, *Russia*, pages 12–13.

238   Hosking, *Russia*, pages 10–11, 21.

239   Robbins, *Travels*, page 45.

240   Peter B. Hammond, *Cultural and Social Anthropology* (London: Mcmillan, 1969), 72–73. Legg, *Barbarians of Asia*, page 46. Jack Weatherford, *Genghis Khan and the Making of the Modern World* (New York: Crown, 2004), page 261.

241   Brown, *Far Traveler,* pages 144–49, 223–36. Ostergren, *Community*, pages 72–102.

242   Michelsen and Rasmussen, page 7–10. Karsten Kjer Michaelsen, "The Teenage Ambassadors . . .," *Danish-North American Relations since World War II* (Ames, Iowa: Danish American Heritage Society, 2004), page 89.

243   Sundbärg, *Sweden*, page 139.

244   Burenhult, *Länkar*, 148–49; same chart in English with an expanded description of women's work: Marie Sørensen, *Gender Archaeology* (Cambridge: Polity Press, 2000), 109–12.

245   Daun, *Swedish Mentality*, pages 137, 135-42. Jonassen, *Values and Beliefs*, page 89.

246   Lintelman, *I Go to America*, pages 78, 98, 105, 110, 134.

247   Lintelman, *I Go to America*, pages 93, 98, 105, 110, 119, 134. Lindström, *Defiant Sisters*. Rasmussen, *New Land*.

248   Claudius Riegler, "Scandinavian Migrants Images and . . .," *Distant Magnets: Expectations and Realities in the Immigrant*

Experience, 1840–1930, Hoerder and Rössler, ed. (New York: Holmes and Meier, 1993) pages 68–72. Rasmussen, *New Land*, page 169.

249 Riegler, *Scandinavian Migrants*, pages 72, 70, et al.

250 Reino Kero, *Migration from Finland to North America* . . . (Turku, Finland: 1974), page 63.

251 Fridtjof Nansen, *Farthest North* (New York: Random House, 1999), pages *xi*, 10–24.

252 Barbara Huck, *Exploring the Fur Trade Routes of North America* (Winnipeg: Heartland Publications, 2001), page 63. Ken McGoogan, *Fatal Passage: The Story of John Rae, The Arctic Hero Time Forgot* (New York: Carroll and Graf, 2002), page 234. Officer and Page, *Fabulous Kingdom*, page 70.

253 Dick North, *The Lost Patrol: The Mounties' Yukon Tragedy* (Vancouver: Raincoast Books, 1995), pages 47–48, 138. Bern Keating, *The Northwest Passage* (Chicago: Rand, 1970), page 65. Charles Officer and Jake Page, *A Fabulous Kingdom: The Exploration of the Arctic* (New York: Oxford University Press, 2001), page 70.

254 Maagerø and Simonsen, pages 80–81.

255 Väinö Linna, "Here Beneath the Northern Star," *Nordic Views and Values*, ed. Patrik Engellau and Ulf Henning (Stockholm: 1984), pages 21–27.

256 Bloch, *Feudal*, pages 88–90, 101.

257 Sundbärg, *Sweden*, pages 312–13, 316. Jonassen, *Values and Beliefs*, page 89.

258 Jenkins, *Sweden and the Price of Progress*, page 19.

259 Borish, *Land of the Living*, page 313.

260 Sahlberg, *Finnish Lessons*, page 96.

261 Kristiansen, *Millennium*, 24. Kristiansen, *Before*, 312–13.

262 Todd, *Making of Modern France*, page 69.

263 *Tacitus*, 1911, pages 92, 95.

264 *Tacitus*, 1911, page 96.

265 Bloch, *Feudal*, pages 114–15.

266   *Tacitus*, 1911, pages 98, 92.

267   Kellogg, "Introduction," page *xlvi*.

268   Snorri Sturluson, *Heimskringla: The Story of Olaf the Holy*, trans. William Morris and Eirikr Magnusson, (London: Chiswick Press, 1894), Vol. II, 118–22, and Brace, *The Norse-Folk*, pages 250–52.

269   Kimmo Katajala, "The Changing Face of Peasant Unrest in Early Modern Finland," *Northern Revolts: Medieval and Early Modern Peasant Unrest in the Nordic Countries*, Kimmo Katajal, editor (Helsinki: 2004), page 161.

270   Haskins, *Normans*. Ingelman-Sundberg, *Boken om Vikingarna*, pages 148–49, 204. Kellogg, "Introduction," page *xlvi*.

271   Fredrik Ström, *Svenskarna i sina ordspråk* [proverbs] (Stockholm: Bonniers, 1926), pages 24, 27, 41. Daun, *Swedish Mentality*, page 179.

272   Esaias Tegner, *Frithiofs Saga*, trans. Locock (New York: Macmillan, 1924), page 20.

273   *Eyrbyggja Saga*, trans. Hermann Palsson and Paul Edwards (Edinburgh: Southside, 1973), page 61. Franklin D. Scott, *Sweden: The Nation's History* (Carbondale: Southern Illinois University Press, 1988), page 62.

274   Sturluson, *Ynglings Saga*, Chapter 2.

275   Aug. J. Thebaud, "History of Ireland," *Northmen in History* (Northfield, MN: Mohn Printing Co). pages 41, 29.

276   Löfgren, *Family and Household*, pages 30–38. Njåstad, *Revolts*, page 95.

277   Steinar Imsen and Günter Vogler, "Communal Autonomy and Peasant Resistance in Northern and Central Europe," *Resistance, Representation, and Community*, editor Peter Blickle (New York: Oxford University Press, 1997), pages 5–6. Njåstad, *Revolts*, pages 111, 114–15. Gustafsson, *Revolts*, pages 29, 31. Johansson, *Revolts*, pages 79, 81–82. Katajala, *Revolts*, pages 14, 160, 195.

278   Katajala, *Revolts*, page 184. Iceland: Juliusson, *Revolts* pages 123–31, 140, 144–46. Denmark: Michelsen and Rasmussen, pages 9–10. Borish, *Land of the Living*, pages 121, 134, 141.

279   Michelsen and Rasmuseen, pages 9–10. Borish, *Land of the Living*, page 143.

280 Katajala, *Revolts*, pages 14, 196–97. Gustafsson, *Revolts*, pages 27–31. Korpiola, *Revolts*, pages 224–25, 228, 251.

281 Todd, *Making of Modern France*, page 175.

282 *Schaff-Herzog*, Vol. IX, pages 417, 419.

283 *Schaff-Herzog*, Vol. IX, pages 417. Roman influence: Bloch, *Feudal*, pages 368–69. Cavalli-Sforza, *Genes*, pages 184–85.

284 Katajala, *Revolts*, page 161. Althusius, *Politica*, IX.

285 Anonymous, *Mirror*, page 81.

286 Katajala, *Revolts*, pages 12–14. Brown, *Far Traveler*, pages 111–12

287 Sundbärg, *Sweden*, page 399.

288 Njåstad, *Revolts*, pages 114–15. Gustafsson, *Revolts*, 19–26.

289 Njåstad, *Revolts*, pages 114–15.

290 Imsen and Vogler, *Community Autonomy*, page 10.

291 Johansson, *Revolts*, pages 54–82.

292 Claes Britton, *Sverige & Svenskarna* (Stockholm: Svenska institutet, 2003), page 16.

293 Njåstad, *Revolts*, page 111.

294 Stefan Persson, *Kungamakt och Bonderätt: Om Danska Kungar och Bönder i Riket och i Göinge Härad Ca 1525 -1640* (Lund: Makadam Förlag, 2005), pages 428, etc.

295 Olsen, *Farms and Fanes*, pages 42–55, 57.

296 Imsen and Vogler, *Community Autonomy*, page 14.

297 Hosking, *Russia*, pages 16–18.

298 Bloch, *Feudal*, pages 49–50, 176–77, 183–88, 243–44, 272–73.

299 Bloch, *Feudal*, pages 49–50, 151–52, 154, 158, 179–80, 247–48, 266, 268–69, 277–79.

300 Sundbärg, *Sweden*, page 142.

301 Peter Blickle, Steven Ellis, and Eva Österberg, "The Commons and the State: Representation, Influence, and the Legislative Process," *Resistance, Representation, and Community*, editor Peter Blickle (New York: Oxford University Press, 1997), pages 336–37. Katajala, *Revolts*, page 199, etc.

302 *Encyclopædia Britannica*, 1902, Vol. XXI, page 26. Bloch, *French Rural*, page 218. Chandler Beach, editor, *The Sudent's Reference Work* (Chicago: F.E. Compton, 1910), Vol. III, page 1638.

303 Maagerø and Simonsen, page 47. Katajal, *Revolts*, page 207. Borish, *Land of the Living*, pages 145–46.

304 Katajala, *Revolts*, page 161. Althusius, *Politica*, IX.

305 Sundbärg, *Sweden,* page 144.

306 Gustafsson, *Revolts*, page 31 (conceptions).

307 Sundbärg, *Sweden*, pages 144, 157.

308 Bloch, *Feudal*, pages 114–15.

309 Blickle et al., *Commons and the State*, pages 122, 336–37.

310 Dr. Richard Andersen, "Chasing the Right *Ting*," *The Danish Pioneer* (Hoffman Estates, IL: Bretelsen Publishing, March 30– April 6, 2009), page 5.

311 Thomas, *Sweden*, pages 27–28.

312 Hosking, *Russia*, page 89.

313 Adolph B. Benson and Naboth Hedin, editors, *Swedes in America* (New Haven, CT: Yale University Press, 1938), page 324. Ingrid Semmingsen, *Norway to America: A History of the Migration*, trans. Einar Haugen (Minneapolis: University of Minnesota Press, 1978), page 141. Hoglund, *Finnish Immigrants*, 115, 135–36.

314 Inglehart, *Human Beliefs*, page 14. Sahlberg, *Finnish Lessons*, pages 97–100.

315 Inglehart, "Culture and Democracy," *Culture Matters*, pages 85, 93.

316 Harrison, *Culture*, page *xiv*. Inglehart, *Human Beliefs*, page 19. de Tocqueville, page 301. Wilkinson and Pickett, pages 238–39.

317 Gjovig and Opstad, page 20. Richard M. Auty, *Sustaining Development in Mineral Economies: The Resource Curse Thesis* (London: Routledge, 1993).

318 Katajal, *Revolts*, page 262. Njåstad, *Revolts*, pages 114–15. Sawyer, *Medieval Scandinavia*, page 172. Bloch, *Feudal*, pages 74–75, 82–85, 87, 101, 247–48 (importance of law).

319 Jonassen, *Values and Beliefs*, pages 29, 33.

320 Bloch, *French Rural*, page 218.

321 Birket-Smith, *Paths of Culture*, pages 35, 37 (Toynbee).

322 Rosander, *Den Nye Skolmästaren*, page 503.

323 Inglehart, "Democracy," *Culture Matters*, page 86.

324 Harrison, *Truth*, pages 94–95. Inglehart, "Democracy," *Culture Matters*, pages 80–97. Inglehart, *Human Values*, pages 4, 15, 17, 20.

325 Seymour Martin Lipset, *American Exceptionalism: A Double-Edged Sword* (New York: W.W. Norton, 1996), pages 77–109.

326 National Opinion Research Center, *General Social Survey* (Chicago: NORC, 1999–2004). Wilkinson and Pickett, pages 53–54. Brookings Institution, Pew's Economic Mobility Project, Opportunity Nation: Rana Forhoohar, "What Ever Happened to Upward Mobility," *TIME Magazine*, Nov. 14, 2011.

327 Jon Gjerde, "The "Would-Be Patriarch" and the "Self-Made Man," Larsen, Bender, Veien, editors, *On Distant Shores: Proceedings of the Marcus Lee Hansen Immigration Conference, Aalborg, Denmark 1992* (Danes Worldwide Archives, 1993), pages 35–49.

328 Marcus Lee Hansen, *The Immigrant in American History* (Cambridge: Harvard University Press, 1940), pages 60–63.

329 Gjerde, "Patriarch", pages 44-45 (stem families).

330 Gjerde, "Patriarch", page 40. Hierarchal society (top-down authority): Betty Wood, *The Origins of American Slavery: Freedom and Bondage in the English Colonies* (New York: Hill and Wang, 1997), page 12, etc. Economic opportunity, prudish, attitude toward Indians: George F. Willison, *Saints and Strangers* (Orleans, Massachusetts, 1945), pages 102–03, 130, various.

331 Lipset, *American Exceptionalism*, pages 19, 79, 109.

332 Finland *jokamiehenoikeudet,* Norway *allemannsrett*, Sweden *allemänsrätt*, Iceland ?.

333 Williams, *American Society*, pages 114–15.

334 E. Adamson Hoebel, *Anthropology* (McGraw-Hill, 1958), pages 499–500. Charles Handy, *The Hungry Spirit: Beyond Capitalism: A Quest for Purpose in the Modern World* (New York: Broadway Books, 1998), page 67. Wood, pages 73, 48, 52-53, 66, 71.

335 Warren Cohen, *Ethics in Thought and Action* (New York: Ashley House, 1995), page 49.

336 Gentile, *Giving Voice*, pages 29–30.

337 Gentile, *Giving Voice*, pages 92–97, 109. Wilkinson and Pickett, pages 197–98. Cohen, *Ethics*, pages 88–89. Handy, *Hungry Spirit*, page 99.

338 David Brooks, *The Social Animal: The Hidden Sources of Love, Character, and Achievement* (New York: Random House, 2011), pages xiii–xiv (character). Gentile, *Giving Voice*, page xxx ("somewhat prepared"), pages 25–27 (rationalizing). Chaffee, *Thinking Critically*, pages 565–66 ("confront authority"). Handy, *Hungry Spirit*, page 99 (Robert Frank).

339 Gentile, *Giving Voice*, pages 25–27.

340 Gentile, *Giving Voice*, pages 24–46. A presentation at Arizona State University (Tempe), Feb. 8–May 25, 2012, "choosing the good" explored how dilemmas (choosing one virtue over another) were viewed in different societies. "Cooperation" was not included on the list of virtues.

341 Maagerø and Simonsen, pages 169, 179. Sahlberg, *Finnish Lessons*, pages 9 (equity), 45 (equity).

342 Karl Mannheim, *Ideology and Utopia,* trans. Louis Wirth, Edward A. Shils (New York: Harcourt, Brace & World, 1936), page 82.

343 Jenkins, *Sweden and the Price of Progress*, page 153. Jonassen, *Values and Beliefs*, pages 13, 18.

344 *The Finnish American Reporter* (Hancock, MI: November 2010), page 21.

345 *The Finnish American Reporter* (Hancock, MI: November 2010), page 21. Borish, *Land of the Living*, page 260. Ulf Nilson, "Aye, Is There Room for a Real Question?," *Nordstjernan* (New York: Nov. 30, 2010), page 13.

346 Ulf Nilsson, "Consensus above All," *Nordstjernan* (New York: March 30, 2011), page 7; and Nov. 30, 2010, page 13. Borish, *Land of the Living*, page 260.

347 Sahlberg, *Finnish Lessons*, page 45.

348 Cohen, *Ethics*, page 77 ("System of thought," "good or bad"). Bethany McLean, Joe Nocera, *All the Devils Are Here:The Hidden History of the Financial Crisis* (New York: Portfolio/Penguin,

2011), page 98 ("blinded" is effectively the same as free from thinking).

349 Inglehart, *Human Beliefs*. Lipset, *American Exceptionalism*, page 26 (moral versus economic).

350 Bloch, *Feudal*, pages 88–93, 101.

351 Lipset, *American Exceptionalism*, pages 18–19.

352 Sahlberg, *Finnish Lessons*, page xx.

353 Frederick Jackson Turner, *The Frontier in American History* (New York: Henry Holt, 1920), pages 263, 261.

354 Cohen, *Ethics*, page 46.

355 Simon Johnson, James Kwak, *13 Bankers: The Wall Street Takeover and the Next Financial Meltdown* (New York: Pantheon, 2010), pages 103, *n*250. McLean and Nocera, *All the Devils*, pages 64, 66, 84-86, 98.

356 McLean and Nocera, *All the Devils*, pages 85-91.

357 Johnson and Kwak, *13 Bankers*, pages 100–01. McLean and Nocera, *All the Devils*, page 85.

358 *Atlas Shrugged* a favorite of ExxonMobil's CEO: Steve Coll, *Private Empire: ExxonMobil and American Power* (New York: Penguin, 2012), page 334.

359 Michael Gerson, "'Atlas Shrugged,' and You Will Too," *Star Tribune* (Minneapolis: April 24, 2011), page OP4.

360 Adam Smith, *An Inquiry into the Nature and Causes of the Wealth of Nations*, 2 volumes (1776) (Oxford: Clarendon, 1976), Vol. 1, pages 26–27. Adam Smith, *The Theory of Moral Sentiments* (Oxford: Clarendon Press, 1976), page 83.

361 Milton Friedman, "The Social Responsibility of Business Is to Increase Its Profits," *The New York Times Magazine*, September 13, 1970. Alternative view (Charles Handy): Mary C. Gentile, *Giving Voice to Values* (New Haven, CT: Yale University Press, 2010), pages 88–89.

362 Smith, *Moral Sentiments*, page 235

363 David Brooks, pages 315–16, 282–87.

364 Gould, *Dinosaur*, page 359.

365 Brizendine, *Female Brain*, pages 18-19.

366 Paul Bloom, *Descartes' Baby: How the Science of Child Development Explains What Makes Us Human* (New York: Basic Books, 2004), page 114, 122. David Brown (*Washington Post*), "Oh, you (empathetic) rat" *Star Tribune*, Dec. 11, 2011, page A20.

367 Smith, *Moral Sentiments*, page 2.

368 J. Kiley Hamlin, Karen Wynn, and Paul Bloom, "Social Evaluation by Preverbal Infants," *Nature* 450 (Nov. 22, 2007), pages 557–59. David Brooks, pages 179, 284. Wilkinson and Pickett, pages 205–06.

369 Wilkinson and Pickett, pages 211–13.

370 David Brooks, page 283.

371 Harrison, *Truth*, page 162. Handy, *Hungry Spirit*, page 65 (Bauman).

372 Ostrom, *Governing the Commons*, pages 35, 88–89, various. Fukuyama, *Culture Matters*, page 108.

373 Handy, *Hungry Spirit*, pages 9–21.

374 T. Harry Williams, Richard N. Current, Frank Freidel, *A History of the United States [to 1876]* (New York: Knopf, 1959), pages 343–48.

375 Wood, pages 12, 96-97.

376 Williams et al., *United States*, page 345 (de Tocqueville). Wilkinson and Pickett, pages 26–27, 163–64.

377 Cohen, *Ethics*, page 184.

378 Minneapolis: *Star Tribune*, January 24, 2003, page B8.

379 Cohen, *Ethics*, pages 157–85. Sabini and Silver, "Critical Thinking and Obedience to Authority," Chaffee, *Thinking Critically*, pages 559–68.

380 Joy Ibsen, "Songs of Denmark," *Danish Culture,* page 365. Borish, *Land of the Living*, pages 238–39.

381 Rauol Wallenberg, *Letters and Dispatches 1924–1944* (New York: Arcade Publishing, 1995), page 48. Borish, *Land of the Living*, pages 223, 237. Gentile, *Giving Voice*: We need to be willing and able to express our values. Chaffee, *Thinking Critically*, pages 565–66. Dorfman, *Thorstein*, pages 3–4.

382 Wikipedia: "Voter Turnout."

383   Inglehart, *Human Beliefs*, page 12 and question A006.

384   Examples: tax cuts for wealthy individuals in the face of widening inequality between rich and poor; price guarantees for pharmaceutical companies in Medicare Part D; tax breaks for long-established oil companies; no indictments of executives in the housing crisis that forced thousands from their homes (including "robo-signing"); protecting the status of health insurers in 2010 health reform legislation.

385   Harrison, *Culture Matters*, page *xiv*. Inglehart, *Human Beliefs*, page 19. de Tocqueville, page 301. Wilkinson and Pickett, pages 238–39.

386   Lipset, *American Exceptionalism*, page 105.

387   Franck, *Summer*, pages 91–92.

388   Wilkinson and Pickett, pages 157–63. National Bureau of Economic Research: <http:www.nber.org/papers/w11253>. Brookings Institution, Pew's Economic Mobility Project, Opportunity Nation: Rana Forhoohar, "What Ever Happened to Upward Mobility," *TIME Magazine*, Nov. 14, 2011. Klein and Rice, *U.S. Education Reform*, pages xiii, xiv, 12–15.

389   Sahlberg, *Finnish Lessons*, pages 48, 114. Wilkinson and Pickett, pages 110–11, 207–09. Brizendine, *Female Brain*, pages 26–28.

390   Britton, *Sverige*, page 17 (16 months total, at least 2 must go to the father).

391   Sahlberg, *Finnish Lessons*, page 10. Wilkinson and Pickett, page 112. Denmark: personal email from David Strand, 1/15/12.

392   Maagerø and Simonsen, pages 169, 179.

393   Sahlberg, *Finnish Lessons*, page 92 (parents), 112 (context, willingness), 42 (ten-year-olds reading—when they start school?). On their own: Lindström, *Defiant Sisters*, page 15. Wilkinson and Pickett, pages 207–09. Brizendine, *Female Brain*, pages 26–28. Susan Mayer, *What Money Can't Buy: Family Income and Children's Life Chances* (Minneapolis *Star Tribune*, September 12, 2012, page OP4).

394   Borish, *Land of the Living*, pages 307–08.

395 Wilkinson and Pickett, pages 177–79. Klein and Rice, *U.S. Education Reform*, pages 9, 25 (same degree of diversity), 40.

396 David Brooks, pages 104–07.]

397 Wilkinson and Pickett, pages 115–16.

398 Williams, *American Society*, pages 115–16.

399 Franck, *Summer*, page 75.

400 Wilkinson and Pickett, pages 173, et al.; Klein and Rice, *U.S. Education Reform*, page 25 (socioeconomic).

401 Organization for Economic Cooperation and Development: *Lessons from PISA for the United States* . . <http:www.oecd-ilibrary.org/educational/lessons-from-pisa-for-the-united-states_9789264096660-en>.. Sahlberg, *Finnish Lessons*, pages 68–69.

402 <http://nces.ed.gov/pubs2011/2011004.pdf>. Klein and Rice, *U.S. Education Reform*, page 24.

403 Klein and Rice, U.S. Education Reform, pages 7–8, 11–12, 47–48.

404 *Folkbildningsförbundit,* 1995.

405 Jonassen, *Values and Beliefs*, page 90. Daun, *Swedish Mentality*, page 176. David Brooks, page 73-74.

406 <http://engtrends.com/IEE/1005A.php>. Klein and Rice, *U.S. Education Reform*, page 10.

407 Wilkinson and Pickett, page 188.

408 PBS Newshour interview with Mattias Rumpf from the Organization for Economic Cooperation and Development, November, 2011.

409 Wilkinson and Pickett, pages 182–83.

410 Wilkinson and Pickett, page 183.

411 Wilkinson and Pickett, page 184.

412 Mette Morsing, Atle Midttun, Karl Palmås, "Corporate Social Responsibility in Scandinavia," page 87.

413 Jenkins, *Sweden and the Price of Progress*, pages 179–80 (Sten Tengelin). Børsen special series on Corporate Social Responsibility; Strand, "Culture and CSR," pages 6–7.

414 Børsen special series; Strand, "Culture and CSR," page 4.

415 "News about Denmark in English," *The Danish Pioneer* (Hoffman Estates, IL: Bertelsen, Jan. 30, 2012), Issue #3, page 2.

416 Anonymous, *Mirror*, pages 80–81.

417 McLean and Nocera, *All the Devils*, pages 85-91.

418 Cohen, *Ethics*, pages 47–49. Milton Friedman, "The Social Responsibility of Business is to Increase Its Profits," *The New York Times Magazine*, September 13, 1970. Gentile, *Giving Voice*, pages xxix–xxx.

419 <http://abcnews.go/Business/states-agree-25b-foreclosure-robo-signing-deal/story?id=1>

420 Turner, *Frontier*, page 32.

421 Inglehart, *Human Beliefs*, A067.

422 Jenkins, *Sweden and the Price of Progress*, page 46.

423 Leena Kurki, "Values, Innovation, Environment Guide to Finnish Companies," *The Finnish American Reporter* (Hancock, MI: August 2011), page 17. Values conflict with marketing: Gentile, *Giving Voice*, page 106.

424 Franck, *Summer*, page 218.

425 Handy, *Hungry Spirit*, pages 26–27.

426 Gentile, *Giving Voice*, page 100 "broader definition."

427 Dorfman, *Thorstein*, page 351.

428 Gjerde, "Patriarch," pages 36–37 (Marcus Lee Hansen, Joseph Schafer). Dorfman, *Thorstein,* page 351.

429 Chaffee, *Thinking Critically*, page 10.

430 Robbins, *Travels*, page 46.

431 Lewis, *Boomerang*, page 15.

432 Dorfman, *Thorstein*, page 350.

433 http://minneapolisfed.org.pubs/fedgaz/03-03/earlychild.cfm

434 TV interview, February 2012.

435 Gentile, *Giving Voice*, page 79 (Baumeister on evil).

436 Sahlberg, *Finnish Lessons*, page 13. Skoglund, *Quiet Courage*, pages 133–35 (appeasement).

437 Sofie Jansson and Katarina Bennich, "The New Media Landscape According to Tomas Brunegård," *Nordstjernan* (New York: May 15, 2011), pages 6–7. David Maki, "Behind the Finnish TV Cameras," *The Finnish American Reporter* (Hancock, MI: Jan. 2011), page 12. Wallenberg, *Letters*, page 48. Franck, *Summer*, page 52.

438 Daun, *Swedish Mentality*, pages 135–42.

439 Inglehart, *Human Beliefs*, question E150. Norwegian students more interested in politics: Jonassen, *Values and Beliefs*, page 33.

440 Wikipedia: "Voter Turnout."

441 Klein and Rice, *U.S. Education Reform*, pages 11–12, 47–48.

442 www.borealforest.org/world/scan_mgmt.htm

443 www.ctba.fr/stodafor/stodafor_project.htm

444 MNForRes-09-Final-Draft.pdf

445 John Platt, "Site Helps Families Protect Woods," *Star Tribune* (Minneapolis: June 30, 2012), page E2. MyLandPlan.org

446 February 7, 2012 interview with Don Mueller, Area Forest Supervisor, MN DNR

447 Turner, *Frontier*, page 290.

448 Inglehart, *Human Beliefs*, pages 12, 14 (cultural maps).

449 As with Feudalism in Denmark, Norway's oil exports have not changed Nordic culture—see cultural maps, Inglehart, *Human Beliefs*, pages 12, 14.

450 Turner, *Frontier*, pages 293, 261.

451 Wilkinson and Pickett, pages 215–28.

452 Dorfman, *Thorstein*, page 340. Wood, pages 54–55.

453 National Bureau of Economic Research: <http://www.nber.org/papers/w112537>. Klein and Rice, *U.S. Education Reform*, pages xiii, xiv, 12-13, 50-51. Wilkinson and Pickett, pages 157–63. Williams, *American Society*, pages 114–15.

454 Turner, *Frontier*, pages 259, 266.

455 In Great Britain: Wilkinson and Pickett, pages 218, 228, 239–40.

456 Klein and Rice, *U.S. Education Reform*, pages 12–13. Wilkinson and Pickett, pages 52, 57.

457 Choice and testing: Sahlberg, *Finnish Lessons*, pages 65–66. Darling-Hammond: Klein and Rice, *U.S. Education Reform*, page 62.

458 Sahlberg, *Finnish Lessons*, pages 101, 103, 105.

459 Handy, *Hungry Spirit*, pages 25–27 (free market). Sahlberg, *Finnish Lessons*, pages 65–66 (choice & testing).

460 Darling-Hammond: Klein and Rice, *U.S. Education Reform*, page 62. Inequality: Handy, *Hungry Spirit*, page 27.

461 Klein and Rice, *U.S. Education Reform*, pages 33–34.

462 Sahlberg, *Finnish Lessons*, pages 71, 74, 76–77.

463 Sahlberg, *Finnish Lessons*, pages 9–10, 72–73, 94–95.

464 Sahlberg, *Finnish Lessons*, pages 41,114.

465 Sahlberg, *Finnish Lessons*, pages 4–7, 41 (opposite), 65–66 (choice and testing don't work), 102 (orthogonal), 105.

466 Daun, *Swedish Mentality*, pages 142–43.

467 Franck, *Summer,* page 92.

468 Cavalli-Sforza, *Genes*, pages 184–85.

469 PBS new report, June 13, 2012.

470 Sally Koslow, *Slouching toward Adulthood: Observations from the Not-So-Empty Nest* (New York: Viking, 2012).

471 Jonassen, *Values and Beliefs*, pages 83, 85, 90. Daun, *Swedish Mentality*, page 176. David Brooks, pages 73–74.

472 Klein and Rice, *U.S. Education Reform*, page 10.

473 Klein and Rice, *U.S. Education Reform*, pages 26–28. Lipset, *American Exceptionalism*, page 117.

474 Jonassen, *Values and Beliefs*, page 83. Lipset and Lenz, "Corruption," pages 119–20.

475 Wilkinson and Pickett, pages 203–07.

476 Bloch, *Feudal*, pages 88–90. Kellogg, "Introduction," page *xxi*.

477 Robbins, *Travels*, page 95.

478 Wallenberg, *Letters*, page 48.

479 Birket-Smith, *Paths of Culture*, page 35.

480 Todd, *Making of Modern France*, pages 68–69. Cavalli-Sforza, *Genes*, pages 184–85.

481 Britton, *Sverige*, page 15.

482 Joy Ibsen, "Songs of Denmark," *Danish Culture*, pages 361-375.

Index